WOLFMAN vs. DRACULA

An Alternate History for Classic Film Monsters

by

Philip J. Riley

Hollywood Publishing Archives

Published by:
BearManor Media
P O Box 71426
Albany, GA 31708
Phone: 760-709-9696
Fax: 814-690-1559
books@benohmart.com

©2010 Philip J Riley
For Copyright purposes
Philip J Riley is the author in the form of this book

Bela Lugosi name and likeness are trademarks of Lugosi Enterprises
Script by Bernard Schubert 1944
Lon Chaney name and likeness are trademarks of Chaney Enterprises
Cover Art - ©2010 By Philip J Riley - Since none of the scripts in this series were thought to exist and were never produced, we have created mock-up posters in the vintage style of the period.
All photographs are from the Author's collection unless noted

The Author would like to thank the following individuals who contributed and helped make this series possible. Carl Laemmle Jr., R.C.Sherriff, Stanley Bergerman, Gloria Holden, Jane Wyatt, Otto Kruger, Marcel Delgado, Robert Florey, Paul Ivano (Cinematographer), Paul Malvern (producer), Elsa Lanchester, Merion C Cooper, Patric Leroux, Bette Davis, Bela G. Lugosi, Sara Karloff, Technicolor Corporation, John Balderston III, Douglas Norwine, Loeb and Loeb Attorneys, David Stanley Horsley, Bernard Schubert, John Teehan

Author's Note: I interviewed the producers, directors, stars, cast and crew in the early to late 1970s. They were recalling events that happened 35-45 years previous and sometimes memory fades or events are recalled from their perspective point of view.

First Edition
10 9 8 7 6 5 4 3 2 1

The purpose of this series is the preservation of the art of writing for the screen. Rare books have long been a source of enjoyment and an investment for the serious collector, and even in limited editions there are thousands printed. Scripts, however, numbered only 50 at the most. In the history of American Literature, the screenwriter was being lost in time. It is my hope that my efforts bring about a renewed history and preservation of a great American Literary form, The Screenplay, by preserving them for study by future generations.

Wolfman vs Dracula

Books by
Philip J Riley

CLASSIC HORROR FILMS
Frankenstein, the original 1931 shooting script
Bride of Frankenstein, the original 1935 shooting script
Son of Frankenstein, the original 1939 shooting script
Ghost of Frankenstein, the original 1942 shooting script
Frankenstein Meets the Wolfman, the original 1943 shooting script
House of Frankenstein, the original 1944 shooting script
The Mummy, the original 1932 shooting script
The Mummy's Curse the original 1944 shooting script (as Editor in Chief)
The Wolfman, the original 1941 shooting script
Dracula, the original 1931 shooting script
House of Dracula, the original 1945 shooting script

CLASSIC COMEDY FILMS
Abbott & Costello Meet Frankenstein, the original 1948 shooting script

CLASSIC SCIENCE FICTION
This Island Earth, the original 1955 shooting script
The Creature from the Black Lagoon, the original 1953 shooting script (editor-in-chief)

THE ACKERMAN ARCHIVES SERIES - LOST FILMS
The Reconstruction of London After Midnight, the original 1927 shooting script
The Reconstruction of A Blind Bargain, the original 1922 shooting script
The Reconstruction of The Hunchback of Notre Dame, the original 1923 shooting script

CLASSIC SILENT FILMS
The Reconstruction of The Phantom of the Opera, the original 1925 shooting script

FILMONSTER SERIES - LOST SCRIPTS
James Whale's Dracula's Daughter, 1934
Cagliostro, The King of the Dead, 1932
Wolfman vs Dracula 1944

AS EDITOR
Countess Dracula by Carroll Borland
My Hollywood, when both of us were young by Patsy Ruth Miller
Mr. Technicolor - Herbert Kalmus
Famous Monster of Filmland #2 by Forrest J Ackerman

FILM DOCUMENTARIES
A Thousand Faces - as contributor (Photoplay Productions)
Universal Horrors - as contributor (Photoplay Productions)

Mr. Riley has also contributed to 12 film related books by various authors
as well as numerous magazine articles and received the Count Dracula Society Award
and was inducted into Universal's Horror Hall of Fame

Wolfman vs Dracula
is Dedicated to:

Rick Baker

Screenplay by Bernard Schubert and Guy Endore

Production Background

Screenplays by Bernard Schubert

The script you are about to read is a copy of screenwriter Bernard Schubert's own script. It was kept in a box in his garage for 40 years when we found it. I had never heard of the title before and he remarked:

"This monster film was to be in Technicolor. You can tell by my script that the sets were few in order to allow for the extra expense of color photography. I was given the script assignment because of my work with Tod Browning and Bela Lugosi on the MGM 1935 film *Mark of the Vampire*.

Bernard L. Schubert was born on January 1, 1895 in Brooklyn New York. After working in many of New York's theater companies he moved to Hollywood in 1931 and immediately got a job at RKO Studios as a staff writer. There he developed his skills and was quickly recognized, although not credited with a film credit until *Fanny Foley Herself*, a 2 tone Technicolor release starring Marie Dressler in 1931, he had written several films with Universal Monster film alumni, David Manners, Helen Chandler, Mae Clarke and J. Carrol Naish.

After his tenure at RKO Schubert worked for Sol Lesser, an independent producer, MGM and Republic. He spent several years in the 1940s at Universal co-writing such melodramas as *Jungle Woman* (1944) and *Frozen Ghost* (1947) and his play *Song of Love*, based on the lives of musicians Robert and Clara Schumann and their relationship with Johannes Brahms was made into a film by MGM in 1947. He tired of studio politics and began a career in early Television production. In the early 1950s he was executive producer of the popular Topper seres from 1953-1955 followed by Crossroads 1955-1957.

"Lon Chaney Jr. was the big horror star at Universal at that time. Kurt Siodmak wrote most of his films and the Wolfman character was his baby. But writing for Technicolor put many restrictions on the writers to allow for the extra expense of color film and in that area I had experience with RKO's *Fanny Foley Herself*. I spent a few hours a week with special effects man David S Horsley trying to visualize just how the black and white monsters would appear in Color.

So my sets included Vasaria, the village, the hospital from *Frankenstein meets the Wolfman* done the year before, the home of the leading lady and her father, the woods and a few rooms in Dracula's Castle. Most of them would use existing sets constructed for the previous monster films.

This film would have been a natural sequel to *Frankenstein Meets the Wolfman* (1943). And the two stars Lon Chaney and Bela Lugosi were to play the lead parts again.

I can't tell you much more about any production background because the production was dropped as Universal only had a six picture and they thought the monsters would carry themselves whereas the Arabian Nights adventure it was changed too would benefit more from the color. And I was assigned *The Mummy's Ghost*, which did make it to the screen"

FILMOGRAPHY OF BERNARD L. SCHUBERT

The Public Defender, Fanny Foley Herself, Secret Service (1931); *Symphony of Six Million*, (1932); *No Other Woman* (1933); *Straight is the Way, Peck's Bad Boy, The Band Plays On* (1934); *Mark of the Vampire* (with Guy Endore), *Kind Lady* (1935); *Hearts in Bondage* (1936); *Make a Wish, The Barrier* (1937); *Breaking the Ice* (1938); *Fisherman's Wharf* (1939); *Scattergood Pulls the Strings* (1941); *Silver Queen* (1942); *Buckskin Frontier* (1943); *Jungle Woman, The Mummy's Curse* (1944); *The Frozen Ghost* (1945); *Song of Love, Song of My Heart* (1947);

As Playwright, *The Schumann Story* (1950)

Television credits:

Mr. & Mrs. North (1952-1954) - executive producer
Topper - (1954) - producer
The Adventures of Falcon (1954) - producer
Crossroads (1955-1957) - producer
White Hunter (1957) - producer
Operation Transfer (1957) - producer
Counterspy (1958) - producer
Key Witness (1959) - producer

Mr. Schubert died in Los Angeles, California on August 4th, 1988 at the age of 97.

David S. Horsley, preparing the special effects on Metaluna in *This Island Earth* (1955)

David Stanley Horsley, ASC Cinematographer was to do the special effects on Wolfman vs. Dracula. He was born on December 23, 1906.

His father, David Horsley opened the very first Studio in Hollywood called Nestor Studios in 1911. But it wasn't until the late 1920s that he moved from actor/electrician to special effects photography and then cinematographer

"I can't tell you too much about this title as I only worked on it for a couple of weeks before it was canned. Being that Dracula met his death in Son of Dracula (1942) and Frankenstein Meets the Wolfman was a big success Universal wanted a sequel with two monsters again. It was first thought that Lon Chaney would play both parts. But then everyone realized that his Larry Talbot would look exactly like his Count Dracula. So Bela Lugosi, who was in his 60s then, was to play Dracula. It was soon realized that he would need a double, as they did in Frankenstein Meets the Wolfman, to do the film, The script called for Dracula to turn into a giant bat and give a big aerial attack at the wolfman in the end scenes. We would have needed a stuntman to accomplish what was written. The flying bat thing had to be done with control wires much like the screenwriter's earlier film Mark of the Vampire (MGM 1935) and it's earlier remake London After Midnight (MGM) 1927.

"The challenges of Technicolor, which had been perfected in 1938-39 didn't present any unscaleable problems, Phantom of the Opera, (1943) made the year before, photographed beautifully, but no one knew how the standard monster character makeup would look with all the extra lighting needed for its proper exposure. Jack Pierce made up Chaney and they shot several poses of him in color in his wolfman makeup. I'm not sure if they experimented on Lugosi but I had not seen any photos of him as Dracula. It was soon after that that I received word that the production was scrapped.

"The monster films remained in B&W and the transformation of Dracula into a bat in later pictures, House of Frankenstein, House of Dracula, and Abbott and Costello meet Frankenstein were all done with cartoon animation. Universal didn't venture into color fantasy films until This Island Earth (1955) for which I did the special effect photography"

David Stanley Horsley spent his last years at the Motion Picture Actor's Home with Larry Fine, from the Three Stooges, as his neighbor. He died on Oct 16, 1976 leaving us a tremendous legacy of photography, special effects, cinematography, inventions and ground breaking techniques.

FILMS OF DAVID S. HORSLEY

The Mystery of Carter Breene, (1915); Freaks, (1932); The Werewolf of London, Bride of Frankenstein, Rough Riding Ranger, No More Ladies (1935); My Man Godfrey, The Lone Wolf Returns, Rose Bowl (1936); Three Love Has Nancy (1938); The Invisible Man Returns, The Boys from Syracuse, The Invisible Woman (1940); The Invisible Agent (1942); Canyon Passage, The Killers, Swell Guy, The Time of Their Lives, Black Angel, Slightly Scandalous, Tangier, Strange Conquest, The Runaround, She Wrote the Book, Singapore, I'll Be Yours (1946); The Michigan Kid, Buck Privates Come Home, Time Out of Mind, Ivy, The Exile, The Senator Was Indiscreet, Brute Force, Something in the Wind, Singapore, Are You with It?, Smash Up: The Story of a Woman, A Double Life (1947); The Countess of Monte Cristo, Casbah, Kiss the Blood off My Hands, Family Honeymoon, All My Sons, You Gotta Stay Happy, Criss Cross, Abbott and Costello Meet Frankenstein, Up in Central Park, One Touch of Venus, Mr. Peabody and the Mermaid, The Saxon Charm, River Lady X, Mexican Hayride, (1948); Abbott and Costello Meet the Killer, Boris Karloff, Jolson Sings Again, City Across the River, Undertow, The Lady Gambles, Once More, My Darling, Francis, Illegal Entry, The Fighting O'Flynn, Woman in Hiding, Johnny Stool Pigeon, Abandoned, The Story of Molly X, Arctic Manhunt, Take One False Step (1949); Commanche Territory, Spy Hunt, Louisa, Buccaneer's Girl, One Way Street, Ma and Pa Kettle Go to Town, Mystery Submarine, Abbott and Costello in the Foreign Legion (1950); Under the Gun, Air Cadet, Target Unknown, Katie Did It, Francis Goes to the Races, Ma and Pa Kettle Back on the Farm, Smuggler's Island, Comin' Round the Mountain, Cattle Drive, Iron Man, You Never Can Tell, The Lady Pays Off, The Raging Tide, Meet Danny Wilson, Abbott and Costello Meet the Invisible Man, (1951); Yankee Buccaneer, Ma and Pa Kettle at the Fair, The World in His Arms, The Black Castle, Against All Flags, (1952); The Strange Door, Abbott and Costello Meet Dr. Jekyll and Mr. Hyde, It Came from Outer Space, City Beneath the Sea, Francis Covers the Big Town, Abbott and Costello Go to Mars, The Glass Web (1953); Magnificent Obsession, Francis Joins the Wacs (1954); This Island Earth, Tarantula, Ma and Pa Kettle at Waikiki (1955); The Ten Commandments, (1956); Jack the Giant Killer, The Longest Day (1962); The Jolly Genie, (1963)

INVENTIONS - Portable remote control devise for Process Projectors, Language translator where an actor's voice can be instantly translated to a foreign language in the actor's actual voice;, Photography transmission process used by NASA in it's early orbital and moon flights and many other new cinematographer's tools still in use today.

ED. There is little more production background that I can add at this point since the only documentation on paper was a memo naming possible Technicolor production in the Universal Central Files and actually viewing one of the color 8x10s of Chaney in his Wolfman test makeup - PJR 2010

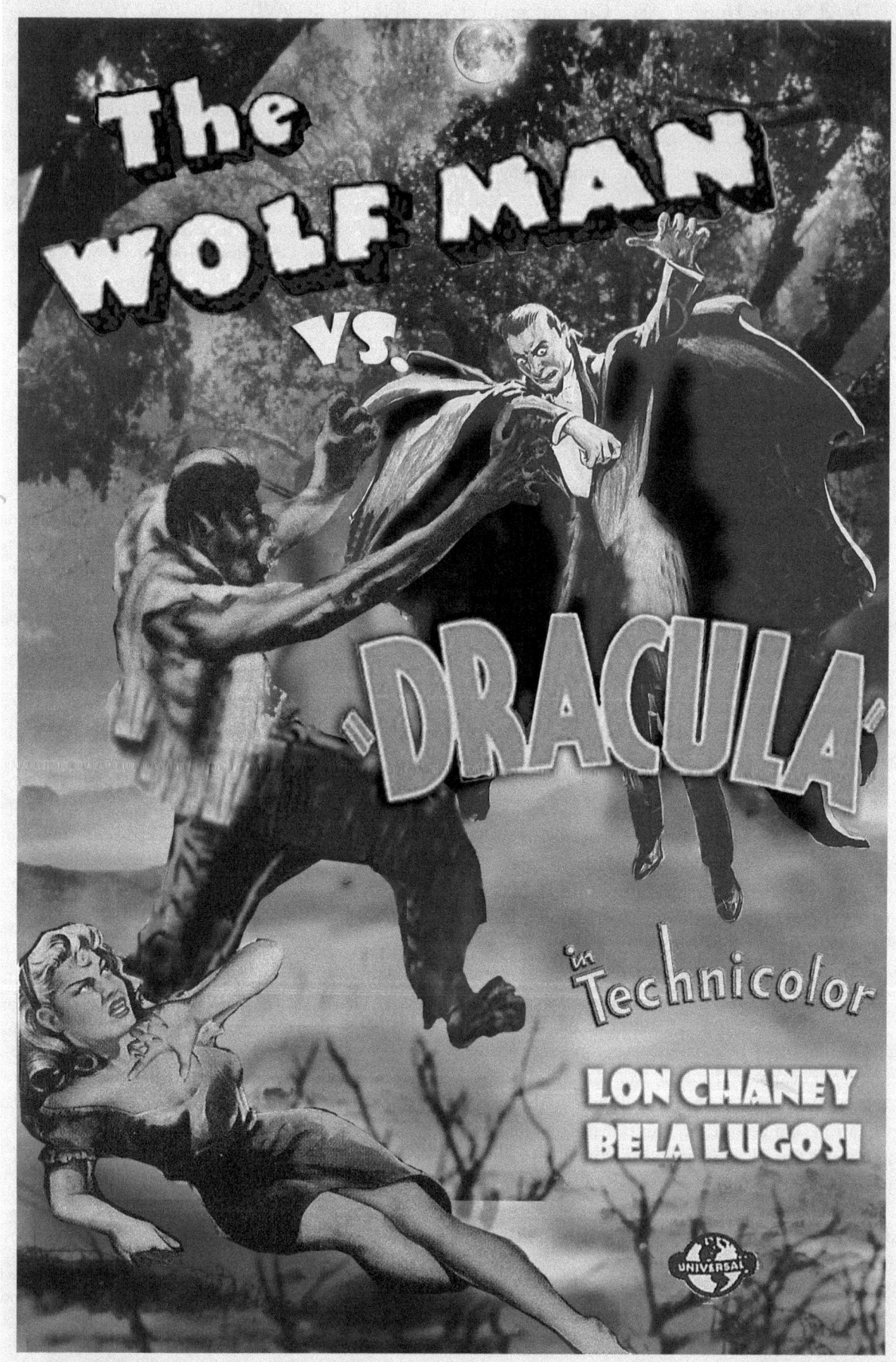

FIRST DRAFT SCREENPLAY
By Bernard Schubert
May 29, 1944

"WOLFMAN vs. DRACULA"

FADE IN:

1.   EXT. SQUARE OF SMALL BOHEMIAN CITY -FULL-NIGHT

   A comprehensive view of the square to show it to best
   advantage. There are only a few people in evidence for
   it is night, and apparently it has been raining for the
   stone paving blocks shine wetly, Two or three of the
   pedestrians still have their umbrellas up. A gendarme's
   slicker, still wet from the recent shower, glistens in
   the light from a window he passes. An old-fashioned car
   stands parked at a curb and a couple of low-swung rigs
   drive through, the horses' hooves clopping; hollowly on
   the pavement.

                                                   DISSOLVE TO:

2.   INSERT - CLOSE

   on a page of a calender for the month of September. Such
   words as appear on it are in Bohemian and the type
   employed is strange as viewed from our concepts. In the
   unnumbered squares at the bottom of the page are shown
   the four phases of the moon. CAMERA MOVES QUICKLY IN to
   the one showing the full moon. The date under it is September 1.

                                                   DISSOLVE TO:

3.   STOCK SHOT OF FULL MOON

   Not far above the line of hills that marks the horizon,
   a few wispy clouds drifting across its face

                                                   DISSOLVE TO

4.   EXT. ROLLING HILL COUNTY - FULL - NIGHT
   The round shouldered hills are fairly heavy with brush
   and on the level stretch at the foot of the slopes are
   tress suggesting a pastorial county. The region seems
   to be beyond the reach of ordinary activities, for there
   is no path and nowhere are there visible signs of human
   habitation.   CONTINUED

4   CONTINUED

Plodding toward Camera from around a foot of the nearest hill, a group of men appear, looming rather grotesquely above the layer of white fog that clings to the damp grassed underfoot. The group is following the lead of an elderly man dressed in peasant costume. He carries a lighted lantern which throws a ghostly halo on the drifting surface of the fog. His eyes are fixed on the ground he traverses. Behind him are a pair of gendarmes wearing the opera bouffe uniform common to south-central Europe. Bringing up the rear, is a heavy-wheeled work cart drawn by a heavy draft-horse of the Clydesdale type. It is driven by a third gendarme, on the seat beside whom rides a doctor in modern dress, his satchel held on his knees. Beside the cart walk two other men in modern apparel, one of whom carries a camera of the Graflex type. These latter two are newspaper men.

As the head of the part nears the CAMERA, it DOLLIES along with the old man and the first two gendarmes. The two uniformed men glance at one another and one speaks rather sourly.

> 1ST GENDARME
> How much farther is it, Novak? Are you going to walk us the full length of Transylvania?

> NOVAK
> (glancing up)
> Oh no, sir. It's not much farther.

He returns his eyes to the ground and gradually comes to a stop, searching the ground rather puzzled. After a moment, a VOICE calls from o.s.

> DOCTOR ZISKA
> (o.s.)
> What are you looking for? Don't tell us you've lost your way!

> NOVAK
> I couldn't have, sir. I left definite markers so I'd surely find it.

He lifts the lantern and peers about on all sides rather bewilderedly - searching for his signpost. He continues just a bit doubtfully:

> NOVAK
> —but the countryside looks no different at night.

5   EXT. COUNTRYSIDE - MED. - <u>NIGHT</u>

at cart. Driver and doctor on seat; the newspapermen on the ground beside it. All are looking forward to where Novak is trying to orient himself.

                      2ND GENDARME
        I'm afraid the old man has led us
        on a wild goose chase, doctor. He's
        too fond of young wine. It's left
        him a bit—

He leaves the line unfinished and with a gyrating forefinger at his temple suggest a warped mind.

                      REPORTER
         (cynically)
        You're probably right. His whole
        story is too fantastic to be the
        truth.

                      DR. ZISKA
        It's too fantastic to be anything
        but the truth. He hasn't enough
        imagination to dream it up.

Then calling ahead to the guide o.s.:

                      DOCTOR ZISKA
        What's the delay, Novak? Something
        wrong?

6   EXT. BRUSHY COUNTRYSIDE - MED - NIGHT

Novak and the two gendarmes on foot in f.g., with the cart and other men vaguely discernible upstage.

                      NOVAK
        No sir. I've found the marker.

He indicates a small pile of stones with a stick on top weighted down with a rock.

                      NOVAK
        It's not far now, sir. Just a
        few yards up the next ravine.

He leads the way out in the direction the stick points. The others follow. CAMERA PANS WITH THE WAGON as it passes.

                                              DISSOLVE TO

7   EXT. RAVINE - MED. FULL - NIGHT

Again the little caravan is approaching CAMERA. Novak's attitude is now changed, He is sure of his ground and is moving more rapidly, his eyes no longer watching the ground, but looking alertly ahead PAST CAMERA. As he and the two gendarmes near CAMERA, it dollies with them for a few feet to bring them to a breast - high shrub that bars their way. Here the old man stops, and pushing the top of the bush aside, raises his lantern to light the terrain beyond as he cries triumphantly:

>   NOVAK
>   There you are, sir ...just as I
>   described it to the police!

The two gendarmes stare off past the bush at something on the ground, their eyes widening in shocked amazement at what they see. Under his breath the first one mutters:

>   1ST GENDARME
>   Mother of mercy!

As the second starts to cross himself, we CU QUICKLY TO:

8   EXT. RAVINE - MED. NIGHT
The doctor, the driver and the two newspapermen are staring off, the doctor and driver rising to their feet for a better view. Whatever they are looking at has a reaction on them similar to what it had on the other gendarmes. The reporter turns incredulous eyes on the cameraman.

>   REPORTER
>   It must be a hoax!
>
>   CAMERAMAN
>   Hoax or not, it's good copy.

Together they start forward. Their action breaks the tension. The doctor and driver jump to the ground and start forward to investigate.

9   EXT RAVINE - MED. FULL - NIGHT
This is shot from reverse angle, cutting above the ground in immediate f.g. so we still do not see what has caused the excitement. Closest to CAMERA are the two gendarmes and Novak who still stands beside the bent shrub, holding his lantern to light his discovery. The newspapermen, the doctor and driver are hurrying downstage from the cart. The pressmen reach Navak first and the photographer raises his camera and snaps a quick flashlight as the doctor reaches him, passes him and kneels to the ground, CAMERA TILTS down with him as he kneels and we get our first glimpse of the cause of their trek.   CONTINUED

9   CONTINUED

Lying outstretched on the ground, the weeds grown up about them, are two inert figures - one, the skeleton of a woman, to judge from the few remaining tatters of clothing left on the bones; the other the figure of a young man in the prime of life. Much of his clothing has also been disintegrated by the elements. Through some bits of cloth still remaining, weeds and grasses have grown - right through the fabric itself. But unlike the girl, the young man appears to be alive - asleep perhaps. His members are well filled and seem firm and his color is quite natural. The fingers of his right hand are entwined with the bones of the girl's left hand. Lying in her widely flung right hand lies a small, badly rusted pistol of old-fashioned design.

Doctor Ziska kneels down beside the man and regards the two figures silently for a moment without touching them.

     DOCTOR ZISKA
   It's just as Novak described it!
   They must have lain here like this
   for years!

During the speech, the reporter has knelt down beside him for a closer look.

     REPORTER
   I still say it's some kind of a
   practical joke!

     DOCTOR ZISKA
   How could it be? You can see how
   the grass and weeds have grown
   straight through what's left
   of their clothing.

     REPORTER
   How could a man lie, dead so long
   and be so perfectly preserved?

     PHOTOGRAPHER
   (kneeling into SCENE)
   Perhaps he isn't dead.

The doctor puts his fingers on the man's pulse and leans over with his ear against his breast. After a moment he straightens.

     DOCTOR
   There is no sign of life.

              CONTINUED

9   CONTINUED - 2

He indicates a clearly visible abrasion on the chest.

                    DOCTOR (CONT'D)
               There's the bullet wound Novak
               told us about.

10   EXT. RAVINE - MED. CLOSE - NIGHT

Novak and the two gendarmes are staring down at the other o.s.

Novak
And there's the weapon that must have made it.

As he speaks he stoops down, CAMERA TILTING DOWN WITH him as he lifts the bones of the skeleton's right hand, in the fingers of which the pistol is clutched.

11   ext. ravine - med. close - night

Doctor and the two newspapermen are looking at the hand of the skeleton.

Photographer
Suicide pact, do you suppose?

Reporter
(heatedly)
How could it be? If they both died at the same time, how could the one be a skeleton while the other remains as if he's asleep?

During this, the doctor's eyes have remained fixed on the body of the man. Now they turn to the other two men curiously. Looking back at the man on the ground, he murmurs half-audibly:

Doctor Ziska
I wonder —

Putting out a hand, he lays it lightly on the exposed upper arm of the man; then he moves it lightly to the throat.

Doctor Ziska (cont'd)
Strange... the flash is not cold...like that of a corpse....

continued

11   continued

His attitude is that of a man speculating on something he even hesitates to admit to himself. Now, as if half fearful to submit himself to a final proof, he tentatively lifts one of the arms at the elbow and with his free hand takes the wrist and bends the arm to test the articulation of the elbow. The arm bends freely! The hand hangs limply at the wrist; the joints of the finger bones are supple, there is no sign of rigidity.

11   CONTINUED

His attitude is that of a man speculating on something he even hesitates to admit to himself. Now, as if half-fearful to submit himself to a final proof, he tentatively lifts one of the arms at the elbow and with his free hand takes the wrist and bends the arm to test the articulation of the elbow. The arm bends freely! The hand hangs limply at the wrist; the joints of the finger bones are supple, there is no sign of rigidity.

> DOCTOR ZISKA
> (with growing amazement)
> There is no sign of life —but there is no indication of rigor mortis either. It is possible that —

He stops short, unwilling to put into words the thought that is struggling for acceptance by his mind.

> REPORTER
>
> Is what possible?
>
> DOCTOR ZISKA
> For centuries science has speculated on the mystery of suspended animation. It is possible that we —
>
> REPORTER
> (interrupting with a laugh)
> Oh, come now doctor! That's a bit to fantastic!

12   EXT RAVINE - CLOSE - NIGHT

The doctor turns quizzical eyes on the speaker o.s.

> DOCTOR ZISKA
> Is it? I wonder.

He lets his eyes turn off into the night as he continues:

CONTINUED

12   CONTINUED

> DOCTOR ZISKA (CONT'D)
> A wiser man than any of us once
> wrote: "There are more things in
> heaven and earth than are dreamed
> of in your philosophy."

Once again he looks down at the body of the man as
he continues:

> DOCTOR ZISKA (CONT'D)
> The fact that we cannot explain
> a thing doesn't give us the right
> to deny it.
>   (then looking up at
>   the gendarmes)
> Jorgen, you and your man lift them gently
> into the cart.

He rises.

13   EXT RAVINE - MED. FULL - NIGHT

The doctor rises and the gendarmes move forward to
obey. He continues speaking while the photographer
snaps another shot of the gendarmes lifting the body
of the man.

> DOCTOR ZISKA
> Back at police surgery we may
> find some means of shedding more
> light on this phenomenon.

As the gendarmes move with their burden toward the cart upstage,

                                              DISSOLVE TO:

14   EXT. CLOCK TOWER - FULL - NIGHT

A trick shot from a still of clock tower against night
sky with full moon double-printed in. The hands on the
illuminated face of the clock show the time to be
approximately six or seven minutes of midnight. As
CAMERA STARTS TO TILT DOWN FROM CLOCK,

                                              DISSOLVE TO:

15   EXT. TOWN SQUARE - (SAME AS IN OPENING) - NIGHT

CAMERA FINISHES TILTING DOWN from clock tower o.s. It
comes to rest on the front of an official looking
building - probably police headquarters in which a
police surgery might reasonably be expected. As
CAMERA TILTS DOWN TO EYE HEIGHT, to establish the front
of the building with lighted doors and windows under
the arcade along the sidewalk, DOLLY IN TOWARD THE
MAIN DOORS, passing thru two or three gendarmes grouped about the
entrance and past a few scattered pedestrians going quietly about the
business. As CAMERA NEARS THE DOOR but while it is still in forward motion,

                                                    DISSOLVE TO:

16   INT. ANTEROOM - MED FULL - NIGHT

It is a rather formal reception room, its architecture
and appointments definitely old-world. It is rather
stiff, its chairs placed at regular intervals along
the walls. The SCENE dissolves thru with CAMERA IN
MOTION, dollying thought a group of some eight or ten
men toward a uniformed man at a broad, heavy flat-
topped desk or table. As SCENE DISSOLVES IN there is
a chorus of ad libs from the men - newspapermen, most
of them probably out-of-town correspondents - some from
foreign papers. They are asking all manner of questions
of the man in uniform who holds eight by ten negative
in his hands. The questions are all to the effect
"Does he really believe it is a case of suspended
animation?" "How does he expect to prove it?" "How
long do we have to wait?" "What is he planning to do?"
etc. etc. As CAMERA NEARS the executive, he holds up
his hands for quiet and says:

                    OFFICIAL

          Gentlemen!   Please - please!

The queries subside. The official smiles and goes on.

                    OFFICIAL
          I realize your papers are anxious
          for details on this strange
          discovery, but the plain truth
          is I know little more about the
          matter than you do.

THE CAMERA HAS COME TO REST during this speech on a
MEDIUM CLOSE SHOT on the official and those of the
reporters nearest to him.

                                                    CONTINUED

16   CONTINUED

                              BRITISH REPORTER
                    Oh, but I say, old man, you cahn't keep us in
                    the dark, you know.

                              OFFICIAL
                         (pleasantly)
                    No, and I can't enlighten you
                    much either, This is an X-ray of
                    the body which Doctor Ziska took
                    immediately it reached the surgery

He holds it out for their inspection. They crowd about it.

17 INSERT CLOSEUP

of X-ray photo of the section of the chest about
the heart, the latter organ being clearly in evidence. One
side of the heart is slightly indented by an object
which is easily recognizable as a bullet of possibly
thirty-eight caliber. As the official talks over the
INSERT, he calls attention to the items mentioned with
the point of a pencil.

                              OFFICIAL
                                (o.s.)
                    The photo reveals a very unusual
                    condition. The bullet from the
                    pistol followed this course. In
                    plain unscientific language, the
                    resistance of the tissues through
                    which it passed regarded its action
                    bringing it to a complete stop at
                    the pericardium or membranous sac
                    in which the heart is suspended.
                    It penetrated neither the membrane
                    nor the heart itself, but lodged
                    against it - as you can see.

18   INT. ANTEROOM - MED. - NIGHT

All inspect the photo and listen with keen interest as
the official continues.

                              OFFICIAL
                    It is Doctor Ziska's theory - mind
                    you, I said theory - that possibly
                    the pressure of the bullet against
                    the heart could have caused it to
                    cease beating - and might thus have
                    induced a condition of suspended
                    animation.

                                              CONTINUED

18 CONTINUED
The local reporter who accompanied the group to the scene of the tragedy, offers a fragment of explanation.

>   REPORTER
>   The doctor believes that by removing
>   the pressure he may be able to
>   restore the - the patient to norm
>   -alcy once more.
>
>   BRITISH REPORTER
>   After all these years? Don't you
>   think he's a bit optimistic, old
>   man?
>
>   REPORTER
>   Possibly - we'll know ore about
>   it shortly. He's in the surgery
>   at the moment proceeding with the
>   experiment.

The last speech is read as the CAMERA LEAVES THE GROUP and DOLLIES TOWARD a closed door on which is lettered in Bohemian:

>   POLICE SURGERY
>   No Admittance.

                                                        DISSOLVE TO

19   INT. SURGERY - MED. FULL - NIGHT

SCENE DISSOLVES IN with CAMERA IN MOTION, DOLLYING UP TOWARD an operating table on which lies the body of the mysterious man who strange condition has caused all the excitement. It is a rather different operating room than the ones we are accustomed to - perhaps a heavy stone arch or similar bit of unaccustomed architecture - to keep us in the foreign atmosphere. Such windows as may be in evidence are quite large and are all heavily barred. Doctor Ziska and an interne are the only characters on stage, the former bent over the still form on the operating table, the interne standing by with his array of instruments and other impediments. CAMERA DOLLIES IN CLOSE enough so that the forms on the table is eliminated just as the doctor straightens with the bullet held in the jaws of a slender probing instrument.

With his eyes still riveted on the form beneath the lamp, the doctor mechanically passes forceps and bullet to the waiting interne with the single word:

                                                        CONTINUED

19   CONTINUED

        DOCTOR ZISKA
    Antiseptic.

The intern lays the forceps on the tray and supplies the antiseptic. Then as the doctor starts applying it to the wound, something about the bullet attracts the interne's attention. Taking it up - still locked in the forceps' grip, he examines it with a puzzled expression.

        INTERNE
    Strange -- this bullet looks home-
    made, doctor. And it isn't lead
    -- it looks more like silver.

        DOCTOR ZISKA
     (not looking up)
    Lead or silver, what does it matter?
    The pressure is removed from the
    heart and ----

He leaves the sentence dangling in mid-air as his fingers reach for the patient's pulse. After a moment he continues as if thinking aloud:

        DOCTOR ZISKA
    --I was a fool even to hope --
    the age of miracles is past --
    this is the age of science -- but --

A look of awe comes suddenly to his eyes as he apparently feels a suggestion of a pulse. He turns his eyes full on the patient's face, hardly daring to believe what his senses tell him.

        DOCTOR ZISKA
    -- but -- do I imagine it, Gustav
    -- or is there a faint sign of
    color returning to his cheeks?

The interne looks more closely at the patient. Apparently he too sees a change in the man's appearance. He says nothing but his eyes widen and he swallows hard. The doctor adjusts a stethoscope and bends over the patient to listen for a heart throb, his head cocked on one side, eyes turned away from the man's face.

20 SURGERY - VERY CLOSE - NIGHT

on patient's face, shooting past the doctor's profile
as he listens for the sound of the heart thru the stethoscope. He does not see as the patient's eyes slowly open. At first their expression is vague, uncomprehending. Then

               CONTINUED

20   CONTINUED

as they become accustomed to the light, they focus
and shift to the doctor and slowly a look of cold hatred
comes into them. In a voice that is barely audible,
but filled with cold venom he says:

> TALBOT
> You are a fool!

The doctor's head jerks around and he stares into the
burning eyes of the patient - dumbfounded - not daring
to believe. For a moment he stares unbelieving, then
slowly pulls back in awe.

21   INT SURGERY - MED. CLOSE - NIGHT

on the three as the awe-stricken doctor slowly draws
himself upright, his eyes fixed on those of the patient
who lies motionless, glaring venomously at him. Instinctively the doctor's hands clutch at the interne's
arm as he half-whispers incredulously:

> DOCTOR ZISKA
> He was dead, Gustav, and I brought
> him back. Do you hear? I have
> brought him back to life!

The last half of the speech is semi-hysterical. Still
lying motionless on the table, Talbot barks a single word.

> TALBOT
> Why?

Doctor and interne stare at his speechless at his unexpect
ed reaction. Then for the first time the patient moves.
Suddenly his arm reaches out and clutches a handful of
his shoulder as he half rises and, thrusting his face
closer to Ziska's, shouts in a voice that is half - plead-
ing and half-rage:

> TALBOT
>
> Answer Me! Why did you do it?

22   INT. SURGEY - VERY CLOSE - NIGHT

on talbot and the doctor as the former glares insanely
at his rescuer. This strange return for what he has done
leaves the doctor nonplussed.

> DOCTOR ZISKA
> You were dead! I brought you
> back to life - and you ask me
> why?

CONTINUED

22   CONTINUED

                    TALBOT
        I was at peace, you mean -- and
        you brought me back to a world
        of torment and despair!
        I ought to --

He stops speaking and in a fury of rage, he twists his hold on the doctor's smock and drags him closer, his intent all too obvious.

23   INT. SURGERY - MED. - NIGHT

on Talbot, doctor and interne. Talbot, still on one elbow on the operating table, has dragged the doctor's face close to his own and is glaring fiercely at him, as he tries to control his rage. The interne quickly interposes, grabbing his hand and trying to disengage it.

                    INTERNE
        Here! Here! This won't do, you
        know! Let him go!

For a moment Talbot retains his grip, the interne being unable to break it. Then of his own accord, Talbot relaxes. His eyes lose their fierce light, his hand releases the doctor and with it he covers his own eyes as if to shut out some horrible picture. The doctor, somewhat shaken, recovers his poise.

                    INTERNE
         (softly)
        Shall I ring for help, sir?

                  DOCTOR ZISKA
        No, no. He'll be all right. It's
        a natural reaction - the shock -
        the excitement, you know.

He lays a kindly hand on Talbot's shoulder.

                  DOCTOR ZISKA
        Lie quiet for a moment. I think
        a mild sedative will help you relax.

                    TALBOT
         (apathetically)
        It's not necessary — I'm all right -
        for the time being anyway.

                                            CONTINUED

23   CONTINUED

As he speaks he turns away from them and lets his head fall back on the table, his face turned away from them. The doctor gives the interne a jerk of the head to follow him and leads the way OUT OF SCENE.

24   INT. SURGERY - MED. - AT A CABINET - NIGHT

On shelves of the cabinet are arrayed small uniform bottles of medicines all properly labeled. The doctor and interne ENTER, the doctor speaking quietly as they come in.

> DOCTOR ZISKA
> (guardedly)
> He'd better have a sedative anyway.

He takes two bottles quickly from the cabinet as he continues:

> DOCTOR ZISKA (CONT'D)
> One dram each in an ounce of warm water. I'll be back in a few moments.

As he speaks he hands the bottles to the interne and EXITS. CAMERA PANS IN to the door thru which he EXITS hurriedly into a hallway, leaving the surgery door open.

25   INT. ANTEROOM - MED. FULL - NIGHT

The reporters previously shown are now moving restlessly about the room or have seated themselves listlessly to wait for the report from the surgery. The British reporter gets to his feet.

> BRITISH REPORTER
> I don't know about your chaps, but I've wasted enough time on a crack-pot theory which —

He stops abruptly as the door is thrown open and the doctor steps in from the corridor. The reporters immediately spring to life and surge forward toward him all asking questions at the same time. He advances to meet them, smiling, triumphant, and holding up his hands for quiet.

> DOCTOR ZISKA
> I can stay only a few moments, but I know you were waiting for a report on my experiment.

CONTINUED

25   CONTINUED

The reporters respond with a volley of question all of the same trend: "Do you mean it worked? Ziska smiles and nods.

> DOCTOR ZISKA
> Yes, gentlemen, my theory was correct. The patient has regained consciousness. He is alive and -- and quite strong.

The doctor's hand instinctively goes to his shoulder where Talbot's hand had grasped it earlier. The remark is received with a series of questions from the eager reporters.

26   SURGERY - MED. - NIGHT

on interne. He stand beside a small retort in a rack above a gas flame waiting for water to heat. He is measuring the liquid from the two bottles into a graduated glass. He turns a Talbot's VOICE reaches from o.s.

> TALBOT (O.S.)
> What phase of the moon are we in?

> INTERNE
> (turning curiously)
> What phase of the moon?

27   INT. SURGERY - MED. CLOSE NIGHT

on Talbot on the table.

> TALBOT
> Yes. When is the next full moon?

28.   INT. SURGERY - MED. - NIGHT

on interne. He looks toward a window o.s. and moves a few paces from the lab table to look out and up.

> INTERNE
> I believe it's full tonight
>   (he cranes his neck to
> look up at it)
> You can't see it at the moment - it's behind a cloud.

With this he moves back to his original position and resumes his work of mixing the potion.

29   INT. SURGERY - VERY CLOSE - NIGHT

on Talbot's face. His eyes stare straight ahead. The facial muscles remain immobile, while slowly his eyes fill with tears. He knows only too well what lies ahead and he is powerless to prevent it. CAMERA DOLLIED BACK to a slightly broader scope and as it comes to rest the o.s. moon comes out from behind the cloud and shining in through the window etches the pattern of the bars across the man on the operating table. Slowly he turns his face toward the source of the moonlight and his eyes roll up toward it.

30   INSERT

A shot of moon through barred window. It has just emerged from behind a cloud.

31   SURGERY - MED. CLOSE - NIGHT

on Talbot. His eyes are fixed on the moon through the window. Silently they turn from the moon to the interne o.s. CAMERA SLIDES IN FAST to a big CLOSE UP of his face. The tears are gone from the eyes now and they are fixed in a maniacal stare on the man o.s.

32   INT. ANTEROOM - MED. - NIGHT

on doctor and reporters who are still clustered about him. They are busily making notes as the doctor speaks.

                    DOCTOR ZISKA
          One of the strangest aspects of the
          case is the patient's reaction to
          being brought back to life. He
          violently resented it - why, I
          have not yet found out.

                    LOCAL REPORTER
          When shall we be allowed to see him?

                    DOCTOR ZISKA
          Certainly not before tomorrow -
          and I cannot even promise that.

33   INT. SURGERY - MED. CLOSE - NIGHT

on interne. He is pouring the warm water into the graduated glass. He disposes of the retort and turns TOWARD CAMERA to carry the concoction to Talbot. CAMERA DOLLIES AHEAD OF HIM His eyes are on the glass as he brushes a few drops of moisture from its surface.

                                        CONTINUED

33 CONTINUED

                    INTERNE
               (as he walks)
          Here you are. Doctor Ziska said
          you should - -

His eyes lift to the o.s. patient and he stops short
leaving the sentence unfinished. What he sees o.s. seems
to have paralyzed his powers of speech. His eyes widen
in horror and his jaw sags... a outcry if abject terror.

34   INT. ANTEROOM - MED. NIGHT
     on Doctor and reporters.

                    DOCTOR ZISKA

               For a time being, gentlemen, you
               must be patient. The important
               thing is: The experiment was a
               success - and soon we —

The speech is interrupted and all on stage a frozen into
immobility by the frightful SOUND of an animal ROAR that
reaches them through the open corridor door. It is
followed by the agonized shrieks of the interne o.s.

                    INTERNE'S VOICE
               (shrieking)
          Help! Doctor Ziska —help- quick —

The SOUND of his VOICE is drowned by the snarls and
gutteral animal growls. For a moment the men stand
paralyzed, then with one accord they spring forward and
rush into the corridor on their way to the surgery to
find out what is happening.

35   INT. SURGERY - MED. FULL - SHADOW EFFECT - NIGHT

     SCENE IS SHOT over some lab equipment in the immediate
     foreground toward a clear space on the white wall of the
     operating room. On the wall is a shadow effect - the
     rectangular outline of an o.s. barred window. Within
     this rectangle is the shadow effect of the Wolfman
     viciously attacking the interne. The latter has ceased
     his shrieks for help and hangs limp and powerless in the
     other's grasp.; Now the Wolfman's shadow is seen to hurl
     the other from him. The interne hurtles into the SCENE,
     strikes the wall and collapses to the floor, out of sight
     behind the foreground table (or other equipment). The
     shadow of the Wolfman remains alone in the outline of the

                                                    CONTINUED

ys

35   CONTINUED
barred window for just an instant, then he is seen (still
in shadow) as he springs to the window sill, wrenches
aside a couple of the heavy iron bars and leaps through to
the outside, leaving the shadow of the window, bars now
twisted half out of their sockets.

36   INT. SURGERY   - MED. -NIGHT

at corridor door. The doctor appears running down the
corridor, followed by the reporters. He stops short in
the open doorway staring off at the interne, the others
massing behind him and staring transfixed for an instant.
One of the number in the rear who cannot see the entire
room, asks sharply.

                    LOCAL REPORTER
            What is it? What's happened?

No one replies, but all move forward toward the interne,
led by the doctor, who kneels beside the victim, speaking
at the same time.

                    DR. ZISKA
            Water and towels - quickly!

One of the men hurries OUT OF SCENE to obey. Ziska continues

                    DR. ZISKA
            That tray of instruments.

A reporter springs to it.

                    LOCAL REPORTER
            Hadn't we better get him up on the
            operating table?

                    DR. ZISKA
            There isn't time! His jugular
            vein has been severed!

                    BRITISH REPORTER
              (looking more closely)
            But how? It wasn't done with a knife!
            It looks more as if it had been torn
            out by - by some sort of wild animal!

                    LOCAL REPORTER
              (looking around room)
            Where is the patient we brought in?

                    BRITISH REPORTER
              (pointing off)
            Look!   CONTINUED

36   CONTINUED

He is staring at the barred window o.s. He and others - all except the one who went for water and the one who brought the instruments - move off toward the window. The Doctor - a part of whom is visible above the foreground table or other masking piece - is busily working over the unseen man on the floor, the other two standing by to be of such assistance as they may be able to offer.

37   INT. SURGERY - MED. - NIGHT

at barred window. The two bars are wrenched apart as the Wolfman left them. The reporters enter quickly and crowd about the window to stare outside as if hoping for a sight of the escaped fiend. There is no sight of him. They draw back and stare incredulously at the twisted bars.

                    BRITISH REPORTER
          How could he have broken those bars?

                    LOCAL REPORTER
          He must have done it with his hands!
          There's no tool in the room he could
          have used!

                    BRITISH REPORTER
          But that's impossible! Not even a
          madman could develop such strength!
          It's superhuman!

He emphasizes the truth of his statement by taking a broken bar with one hand and trying to bend it. It is as rigid as a tree trunk. The action is halted by the long, haunting wail of a wolfman somewhere outside. The men listen intensely, their eyes searching one another's faces.

                    BRITISH REPORTER
               A wolf cry!

                    LOCAL REPORTER
          There hasn't been a wolf in this
          region in a generation!

The look off toward the doctor as they hear his voice o.s.

                    DR. ZISKA
          Gustav is dead!

They move out towards the speaker.

38 INT. SURGERY - MED. FULL - NIGHT

SHOOTING OVER lab equipment as previously so as not to show the mangled body of the victim on the floor. The doctor is rising to his feet, his eyes still fixed on the victim. His expression and those of the remaining two reporters reflect the gruesome sight on the floor.

> DR. ZISKA
> What a horrible way to go --
> literally torn to pieces by the
> man he had just helped restore
> to life!

Then as the other reporters move quietly INTO SCENE he looks up at them and continues:

> DR. ZISKA
> Phone your papers! Get to the police!
> Warn the countryside! A homicidal
> maniac is at large and must be hunted
> down like a wild beast!

As the reporters move to attend to this, the wolf HOWL is HEARD for the second time, chilling them to the bone and causing them to search one another's faces for an explanation of the horror that seems to ride on the wailing cry.

FADE OUT

FADE IN:

39 EXT. WOODS - FULL - DAY

CAMERA sits in the middle of a small stream and is SHOOTING ALONG its course to where it disappears under low, overhanging brush. It PANS AND TILTS DOWN to a dark pool at the stream's edge. In its glassy surface is seen the reflection of Talbot as he approaches the stream with a backward glance as if fearful of pursuit. He is dressed differently from the way we last saw him. The clothing - stolen perhaps - are rough but whole. The rags and tatters in which we first saw him he carries rolled into a bundle. He pauses at the stream's edge and kneeling beside it, peers at his reflection in its surface. Now he spreads his hands before him staring at them at them as if to see whether they still bear any semblance to the hairy, wolfish appearance they had taken on the night before. Now over-come by a sudden wave of agony at his recollection of
the night's happening, he buries his face in his hands.
CAMERA TILTS UP to him. For a moment he remains
CONTINUED

39 CONTINUED

thus, then starts washing his hands as if to cleanse them of their crime. Now he takes up a boulder from beside him and, wrapping the discarded clothing about it, starts to wade into the water.

40 EXT. WOODS - MED. - DAY

on Talbot, SHOOTING ACROSS the stream. He wades into the water, finishing wrapping the clothes about the boulder. In midstream he stops and sinks the bundle to the bottom of the stream where it is not likely to be found for a time. As he splashes on toward CAMERA it DOLLIES BACK with him.

LAP DISSOLVE TO:

41 EXT. WOODED HILL ROAD - MED. - DAY

on Talbot as he climbs an easy slope to the road, CAMERA DOLLYING BACK with him at same speed of previous scene. Gradually the DOLLY SLOWS DOWN and PANS with him to show him pause at a sign post beside the road on which is easily read: SLAVNO 132 kilometers. A hand or arrow points in the direction Talbot is moving. With CAMERA IN MOTION

DISSOLVE TO:

42 EXT. STREET IN SLAVNO - MED. PAN AND DOLLY - DAY

on Talbot as he moves along the street and heads out through the city's gates toward open country. As CAMERA FOLLOWS him.

FADE OUT

FADE IN:

43 EXT. ROAD NEAR ANATOLE'S FARM - NIGHT

The farm buildings sit on the summit of a small, round-topped hill surrounded by other and higher hills. Except for those buildings and the masonry wall surrounding them, there is no other sign of human habitation, giving the place a feeling of loneliness and isolation. The scene dissolves in with the CAMERA IN MOTION, DOLLY WITH Talbot as he approaches the crudely arched gateway to the compound. The FORWARD MOVEMENT of the CAMERA brings it to a point which lets us see through the gateway and gives us our first view of the compound, an unusual and interesting picture of peasant life. Along the left

CONTINUED

43   CONTINUED

wall is a crude shelter for a couple of cows and a team of draft horses. On a stanchion near the cows hangs a lantern although no one is seen within it's circle of light. At the far end of the compound stands the owner's cottage, its windows cheerily lighted from within. Talbot comes to a stop in the gateway surveying the picture, seemingly unable to decide whether to go on to the house. Now he takes a couple of backward steps and drops wearily on a wooden barrow standing at the edge of the gateway, his head in his hands. Now into the light of the lantern near the cows a girl ENTERS and starts to take it down from its peg.

44   EXT. COW SHELTER - MED. - NIGHT

The girl (Yvonne) is taking down the lantern with one hand while with the other she carries a wooden bucket partly filled with milk. A one-legged milking stool is tucked under her arm. She is a drab peasant type, colorless and with lifeless eyes. Her clothes are of a lifeless gray and over her head she wears an unbecoming kerchief of the same unattractive color. Removing the lantern, she moves away from the cow she has just milked and moves around to the second one. As she starts to hang the lantern on a post nearby, CAMERA MOVES QUICKLY IN to a CLOSER view of her. She stands a moment looking off uneasily toward the house. CAMERA SWINGS OFF her TOWARD the house at the far end of the compound as the figure of a man in the silhouette moves to one of the lighted windows and stands looking out into the yard.

DISSOLVE TO

INT. FARM KITCHEN - MED. - NIGHT

45

at window. Anatole (Yvonne's father) stands at the window looking out into the yard toward where the girl is milking. He is a peasant and is dressed in typical farm clothing, but very clean. He is clean shaven and has an intelligent, kindly face. The kitchen, like those of most peasant homes is rather more than a mere kitchen. It is also the dining room and general living room. Its floor is of flagstone and it is simply but cheerfully dressed. It's chief feature is the big, deep fireplace which serves for cooking as well as a source of warmth. A huge iron kettle hangs from a crane imbedded in its bricks. Along one wall a short flight of steps climbs to a landing where a closed door suggests a continuation of the stairs leading to sleeping rooms above. The alcove formed by the underside of the steps forms the actual kitchen portion of the room, which is indicated by the rows of shining pewter and copper utensils above a work

CONTINUED

45 CONTINUED

    table. In the center of the room there is a heavy general utility table and against one wall stands a character piece, a combination desk and book cabinet above with a small mirror set against the back wall of the desk portion. Anatole turns from the window and CAMERA PANS HIM to the fireplace bringing into scene a larger portion of the room. Count Dracula sits with his back to the camera beside the big table. A dark china shade on the table lamp throws his head into shadow. He wears an old-fashioned, black cape coat and beside him on the table lies his flat-crowned, limp-brimmed black hat. He does not look up as Anatole crosses to fireplace, speaking as he walks.

> ANATOLE
> I am not unmindful of the honor you do my daughter, but surely, Count Dracula, a man of your position would find a more suitable wife among the women of your own class.

By the end of the line, Anatole has reached the fireplace and is leaning against a corner of it facing the Count. He is rather uncomfortable, unwilling to offend his visitor yet not too pleased at the thought of his offer of marriage. The Count does not move as he replies quietly

> COUNT DRACULA
> My dear Anatole, let me be the judge of that. Properly groomed, Yvonne would be a credit to any class.

> ANATOLE
> I am hardly the one to doubt your judgement - and yet she has never had a suitor.

> DRACULA
> (quietly)
> That's not because of your - shall we say - profession?

> ANATOLE
> I dare say you're right

> DRACULA
> Well, do you want her to live and die a spinster?

                                                CONTINUED

at

45   CONTINUED - 2

                    ANATOLE
            Of course not.

                    DRACULA
            If no one wants to marry her
            while she's young, will anyone
            want to when she's old?

                    ANATOLE
            I suppose they won't.

                    DRACULA
                (persuasively)
            Then what are your objections
            to me?

46   INT. KITCHEN - MED. CLOSE - NIGHT
      on Anatole. He looks quickly at the doctor, apparently
      anxious to avoid offending him.

                    ANATOLE
            I have no personal objections,
            Count. But I - I Can't answer
            for Yvonne.

47   INT. KITCHEN - CLOSE - NIGHT

      On the Count. This is the first time we have seen him
      except from the back. His face, shaded from the light
      of the lamp behind him, is almost in silhouette as he
      leans quickly forward and speaks angrily.

                    DRACULA
            Why not? Why should she object?
            Does she think I'm not good enough
            for her - a peasant girl - the
            daughter of a --

48   INT. KITCHEN - CLOSE - NIGHT

      on Anatole

                    ANATOLE
                (interrupting)
            It's not that - really! It's only
            that she's a girl of strong religious
            convictions and she feels that you
            are -- well - a

                                              CONTINUED

48   CONTINUED

He comes to a faltering halt unable to find a word that will not offend.

                    DRACULA
          A heretic, perhaps?

                    ANATOLE
          I'd hardly say that, Count.

49   INT. KITCHEN - MED. CLOSE - NIGHT

on Count.

                    DRACULA
          Why not? Anyone not of your own
          faith is always a heretic.

He laughs cynically, then continues:

                    DRACULA
          Religion - bah!

He rises and CAMERA PULLS BACK to include Anatole as the doctor paces up and down past him as he continues his diatribe.

                    DRACULA
          Most of it belongs back in the
          Dark Ages where it came from -
          along with the belief in demons
          and werewolves and vampires.

He stops shortly and turns to Anatole.

                    DRACULA
          I hope I don't offend you. Perhaps
          you believe in such things yourself.

                    ANATOLE
          Nonsense.

He smiles and continues:

                    ANATOLE
          But I know men who do - and who
          claim there is proof that these
          hills were once infested by the
          undead.

at

50   INT KITCHEN - TWO SHOT - DIFFERENT ANGLE - NIGHT

The Count moves to a conspicuous place before the fire as he replies.

> DRACULA
> Of course - and all because a man once lived here whom they feared - an ancestor whose title I bare a Count Dracula. Fearing him, they invented malicious tales about him - claimed he was one of the undead... a vampire that roamed the countryside at night and subsisted on blood which he drew from the throats of the living victims. A being of solid substance like ourselves who could be touched and seen - but who cast no reflection in a mirror.

Toward the end of this speech, CAMERA SWINGS from the two men toward the mirror in the desk-bookcase-cabinet and now DOLLIES QUICKLY up to the mirror at an angle to show the front of the fireplace - only in the mirror only Anatole stands in the scene. The Count is not visible in the mirror, but his voice continues. CAMERA MOVEMENT is timed so that as the reflection comes into CAMERA, the Count's voice is saying: "...but who cast no reflection in a mirror." His voice continues:

> DRACULA
> (invisible in mirror)
> What utter nonsense! He could change his form from a man to a bat, or a wolf, or a thin wisp of vapor, so they said -- and the only protection against him was a crucifix.

During the speech CAMERA SWINGS BACK from mirror to fireplace.

52   INT. KITCHEN - SAME SET UP - NIGHT

as previous scene. The Count is now in position before the fire and can't be seen in the mirror. SWING CAMERA from mirror to fireplace where we see Dracula and Anatole standing as before. Scene 50 and 51 are CUT TOGETHER on CAMERA SWING to give illusion we have panned from the mirror in which he doesn't register to the scene where he presumably has been standing all the time. His voice has continued without pause during all this.

CONTINUED

at

51   CONTINUED

                    DRACULA
          But powerful as he was by night
          he had to spend the daylight
          hours in his coffin and he could
          only be destroyed by finding
          him there and driving a stake
          through his heart!

CAMERA HAS MOVED SLOWLY IN to a tight TWO_SHOT, favoring
the Count who regards Anatole narrowly as he continues:

                    DRACULA
          Is it possible Yvonne thinks I
          am of the same clan - because I
          bought his tumble-down castle
          and rebuilt a few of the rooms
          for my quarters.

                    ANATOLE
          My daughter is not a complete
          fool, Count.

The Count's face relaxes into a thin smile.

                    DRACULA
          Then tell her of my proposal.

He crosses to the table and takes up his hat, Anatole
following. As the CAMERA PANS THEM to the door the
doctor continues speaking.

                    DRACULA
          You might also tell her I need
          not be a heretic, merely because
          my philosophy differs from hers.
          I'll stop by for her answer
          sometime tomorrow. Goodnight.

Anatole wishes him goodnight and closes the door behind
him.

52   EXT. COMPOUND - MED. - NIGHT

The Count is walking away from the house. He comes to
a stop in f.g. and looks off toward the cow shelter, a
thin smile coming to his lips. With a quick glance
back toward the house, he EXITS toward the sheds.

at

53 INT. COW SHELTER - MED - NIGHT
on Yvonne as she rises from milking the second cow.
She sets the bucket aside and turns away to put up the
milking stool. The Count ENTERS quietly and steps behind
her. As she turns to pick up the bucket she sees him for
the first time and starts back with a little exclamation
of alarm.

                        DRACULA
            Forgive me if I startled you. I
            only stopped to say goodnight.

Yvonne recovers from her little fright and replies with
a smile.

                        YVONNE
            Goodnight Count Dracula.

She stoops to take the bucket but he stops her with a
light touch on the shoulder.

                        DRACULA
            Before I go - your father has
            given his consent to our marriage.

For a moment the girl looks at him blankly, the asks:

                        YVONNE
            Does that mean I have no choice in
            the matter?

The Count smiles quietly and shakes his head.

                        DRACULA
            Your father said you had no other
            suitor.
                        YVONNE
            (dropping her eyes)
            I haven't - but -
                        DRACULA
           (interrupting)
            Then what have you to choose
            between.

He produces something from a pocket and continues:

                        DRACULA
            Look - -I've brought you a little
            engagement present.

He holds out toward her a long rope of pearls. Yvonne
stares down at it incredulously.
                        YVONNE
            (in a half whisper
            Oh - they're lovely!

                                                                 CONTINUED

at

53 CONTINUED - 2
She reaches for them, then draws back her hand involuntarily and closes her two fists against her breast.

54 INT. COW SHELTER - CLOSE NIGHT
on Yvonne, hands clasped at her breast as she continues her speech.

>   YVONNE
> Too lovely for - for anyone like me!

55 INT. COW SHELTER - CLOSE - NIGHT
on Count as he smiles and shakes his head.

>   DRACULA
> You're mistaken, my dear - as you'll see when you try them on before your mirror.

56 INT. COW SHELTER - MED. NIGHT
on the two. As the Count ends his line he extends the pearls toward the girl. She hesitates, glances up at him, then timidly takes them and lets them pour through her fingers like drops of milk. The Count watches her appraisingly for a moment, the says, quietly inviting:

>   DRACULA
> Or perhaps you'd try them on now - for me.

Yvonne's eyes search his face quickly. Then:

>   YVONNE
> Now? Why, yes - of course - if you like.

She lifts the string of jewels as if to loop them about her throat, but the Count stops her gently.

>   DRACULA
>   (smiling tolerantly)
> One doesn't wear two necklaces at the same time, child. First remove the pendant you're already wearing.

>   YVONNE
> That's my crucifix!

Instinctively her hand clutches at the cross where it hangs under the yoke of her peasant's dress. (Note: Throughout all the foregoing, the cross is at no time visible, otherwise - according to folk lore, the Count would not be able to remain.

CONTINUED

56 CONTINUED

>   DRACULA
>   The metal chain will spoil the
>   effect. Surely you can see that.
>
>   YVONNE
>   No, not exactly, but-
>
>   DRACULA
>   (quickly)
>   But you will take it off, won't you?

57 INT. COW SHELTER - CLOSE - NIGHT

on Count. His eyes grow hard and are fixed unblinkingly with a hypnotic stare on the girl's o.s. as he continues speaking slowly and impressively:

>   DRACULA
>   Only for a moment - just to please
>   me. I - am - sure - you - will.

58 INT. COW SHELTER - MED. CLOSE - NIGHT

on Yvonne over Count's shoulder. She is staring into his eyes as he finishes the last portion of his last speech. After a moment her eyes take on somewhat the expression of a sleepwalker's and she replies in a quiet monotone.

>   YVONNE
>   Why, yes. I - I see no harm
>   in that.

Still staring into the Count's eyes, her hands lift mechanically to the nape of her neck and she starts fumbling at the chain's clasp.

>   DRACULA
>   (barely audible)
>   And when you have removed it,
>   drop it behind you.
>
>   YVONNE
>   Yes - - of course.

Suddenly the blank look leaves the girl's eyes and both she and the Count look quickly o.s. as Talbot's VOICE is HEARD

>   TALBOT'S VOICE
>   I beg your pardon!

59 INT. COW SHELTER - MED - NIGHT
on Count, Yvonne and Talbot who obviously has come up unnoticed toward the end of the foregoing scene with out suspecting its meaning. Before either of the other two can speak, Talbot continues his speech.

> DRACULA
> Is this the home of Anatole Ponowiecz?

For just a split second neither of the others answers, then the inwardly raging Count snaps:

> DRACULA
> It is - but you've come at a most inopportune time, my friend.

Talbot's whole bearing bespeaks weariness to the point of exhaustion.

> TALBOT
> I'm sorry to disturb you, Herr Ponowiecz. But I've come such a long way, you've got to let me talk with you.

> DRACULA
> I'm not Herr Ponowiecz, and if I were I'd have no time to waste on tramps. Now suppose you leave the way you came.

60 INT. COW SHELTER - CLOSE - NIGHT
on Talbot. He bristles at the Count's attitude and for a moment he forgets his fatigue.

> TALBOT
> It might be fun to slap a little common courtesy into a fellow like you - - -

61 INT. COW SHELTER - MED. - NIGHT
on the three. The Count stiffens at Talbot's remark, but the latter runs a hand wearily over his face and continues:

> TALBOT
> - but I'm too tired to quarrel.

CONTINUED

at

61   CONTINUED
He turns to Yvonne.

> TALBOT
> Maybe you'll tell me where to
> find the man I'm looking for

> YVONNE
> I'll take you to him. He's my
> father.

She takes up the milk bucket from the ground and
reaches for the lantern. Talbot steps to her side
and relieves her of the pail, leaving her the lantern.

> YVONNE
> Goodnight Count Dracula

The Count bows gravely and as the others START OUT
speaks:

> DRACULA
> Remind you father I'm to see him
> tomorrow.

Yvonne throws him a quick, worried look.

> YVONNE
> I shan't forget.

She EXITS with Talbot. CAMERA DOLLIES IN CLOSE on the
Count who stands looking narrowly after them.

62   INT. KITCHEN - MED. FULL - NIGHT

Anatole is disc. pacing rather moodily about the room.
On the opening he is walking upstage toward the fireplace. The door downstage opens and Yvonne steps in
carrying the lantern. Talbot is far enough behind her
so that as Anatole glances around he fails to see him.
He moves on toward the chimney, but turns sharply as
Yvonne speaks.

> YVONNE
> There's a gentleman here to see
> you, father.

As Anatole turns with more than normal surprise, Talbot
steps into the room and closes the door. The girl takes
the milk bucket from him and EXITS toward the kitchen
alcove. CAMERA DOLLIES with Talbot as he walks upstage
to Anatole who stands watching him curiously. Anatole
is not sullen, nor surly. He is only quite frankly
amazed at receiving a visitor and shows it. As Talbot
approaches him, he asks:
                                                CONTINUED

at

62 CONTINUED

          ANATOLE
       (incredulously)
  You have come here - to see me?

          TALBOT
       (wearily)
  Yes.

He draws a hand across his forehead and continues:

          TALBOT
  May I sit down? I've walked a
  good many miles since sunrise.

Anatole waves him to a seat. Talbot drops into it, rests an elbow on his knee and leans his head in his hand tiredly. Anatole regards him speculatively.

63 INT. KITCHEN - CLOSE - NIGHT
on Anatole.

          ANATOLE
  You must be a stranger in this
  district.

64 INT. KITCHEN - CLOSE - NIGHT

on Talbot. Something in the older man's tone causes him to life his head and regard him curiously.

          TALBOT
  Why do you say that?

65 INT. KITCHEN - MED. NIGHT
on the two men - at an angle that includes the kitchen alcove upstage where Yvonne is busy straining the milk into shallow pans. Anatole glances at her before replying.

          ANATOLE
  People who know us generally avoid
  us - because of my occupation.

Talbot lowers his head and runs his fingers wearily through his hair as he replies listlessly.

          CONTINUED

65   CONTINUED

> TALBOT
> Yes, I am a stranger. I'm English. My name is Larry Talbot.

Now he looks up quickly - almost defiantly.

> TALBOT
> But I do know who you are!

> ANATOLE
> You do?

> TALBOT
> (nodding)
> I stopped in Slavne and looked you up. You're Anatole Ponowiecz - Anatole, the hangman.

Anatole smiles. Now he understands.

> ANATOLE
> I see. You're here on official business.

> TALBOT
> Yes, I suppose I am, in a way. But I -

He glances at Yvonne before continuing to Anatole:

> TALBOT
> It would be easier to explain if we were alone.

> ANATOLE
> (glancing at girl)
> Yvonne.

Without looking up she replies quietly.

> YVONNE
> Yes, father.

taking up the lantern she EXITS toward the stairs Talbot's eyes following her. He rises from the chair and speaks to her.

> TALBOT
> I'm sorry, Miss. Please don't think I mean to be rude.

at

66 INT. KITCHEN - MED. - NIGHT

at stairs. Yvonne is nearing the landing. She stops with a hand on the knob of the door and answers with a smile.

                         YVONNE
              I don't. Goodnight.

She EXITS on her way upstairs closing the door behind her.

67 INT. KITCHEN MED. - NIGHT

on the two men. Talbot is looking after the girl.

                         ANATOLE
              You came to me, the hangman - why?

Talbot turns and regards him silently for a moment, then he says simply:
                         TALBOT
              Because I want to die.

For a moment Anatole stares nonplussed.

                         ANATOLE
              Nonsense. No man wants to die.
              I know!
                         TALBOT
              I do! It's the only hope I've got
              left - death - as quick and as sure
              as you can make it! You will do this
              for me, won't you!

In his eagerness to sell his point, he has stepped closer to Anatole during the speech and by the end is gripping his arm with one hand while he stares into his eyes pleadingly - hopefully.

68 ING. KITCHEN - CLOSE - NIGHT

on Anatole. He stares off at Talbot incredulously.

                         ANATOLE
              But, my dear boy, I can't do what
              you ask. It would be murder!

69 INT. KITCHEN - CLOSE - NIGHT
    on Talbot.
                         TALBOT
              Why? Why is it worse to kill a
              man who wants to die then it is
              to have some poor devil who wants
              to live?

70 INT. KITCHEN - MED. - NIGHT
    on the two men

                    ANATOLE
           It is the State that hangs men -
           not I. My part is as impersonal
           as the rope that sends them kicking
           into eternity.

                    TALBOT
           What's the difference? They're just
           as dead, aren't they?

                    ANATOLE
           The difference is that, hangmen
           though I am, I'm a God-fearing
           man. I couldn't kill as one man
           kills another. You can understand
           that can't you?

                    TALBOT
                (hopelessly)
           I suppose so - but what happens
           to me? I can't go on this way
           knowing what lies ahead - watching
           it come closer and closer, day by
           day until.

He leaves the line unspoken and dropping into his seat,
buries his face in his hands - the picture of despair.

71 KITCHEN - CLOSE - NIGHT

on Anatole. He looks compassionately at Talbot.

                    ANATOLE
           What is it, son? Some incurable
           illness?

72 INT KITCHEN - CLOSE - NIGHT
    on Talbot, seated and his head in hands.

                    TALBOT
           No - - or maybe it is, but not
           the way you mean. I'm a murderer.

He lifts his head and stares up into Anatole's eyes o.s.

                    TALBOT
           A murderer!

He rises and clutches Anatole by the arms, CAMERA TILTING
UP with him to a tight TWO-SHOT as he continues:

                                        CONTINUED

72 CONTINUED

> TALBOT
> I kill and kill - not because I
> want to but because I can't help
> it!

He lets go of the older man and continues his speech as he walks upstage.

> TALBOT
> A week ago I killed a man - a man
> I didn't even know - a man who was
> trying to befriend me! And it will
> happen over and over again!

He ends with back to camera and his face buried in his hands as if to shut out the thought

> ANATOLE
> Why not surrender yourself to the
> law and -

Talbot whirls round facing him and interrupts wildly.

> TALBOT
> The law won't help me! And do you
> know why?

He comes back quickly on the line and faces Anatole who shakes his head no.

> TALBOT
> Because I can only be killed by a
> silver bullet - and the law won't
> believe that!

> ANATOLE
> A silver bullet! That sounds a bit
> mad, doesn't it?

> TALBOT
> Does it?

He rips his shirt open, exposing his chest to the other.

> TALBOT
> Do you see that mark? Do you
> know what it is?

73 INT. KITCHEN - CLOSE - NIGHT
on Anatole. He lifts his eyes from the mark to Talbot.

> ANATOLE
> It is a pentagram - a five pointed
> star, drawn inside a circle!

74 INT. KITCHEN - CLOSE - NIGHT
on Talbot as he covers the mark without the camera having seen it.

>TALBOT
>It's the mark of the Beast! The brand of the werewolf! I can even see it in the hand of the person marked as my next victim! They can't but I can!

75 INT. KITCHEN - MED. - NIGHT

on the two.

>ANATOLE
>You don't need a silver bullet, son. What you need is a doctor.

>TALBOT
>I know! You think I'm mad, don't you?

>ANATOLE
>Frankly I do. There are men who believe they turn into animals at certain phases of the moon...but it's all in their minds!

>TALBOT
>It's all right for you to say that! But I've seen my victims afterwards and they were ---

Again he drops into the chair

>ANATOLE
>I don't deny that you may become violent. But there's no such thing as a werewolf - and madmen can be cured.

>TALBOT
>(to himself)
>If it were only as simple as that!

>ANATOLE
>Believe me, it is. Tomorrow we'll have a talk with Count Dracula He's one of the finest --

>TALBOT
>Dracula! I met him in your yard tonight, He wouldn't help me even if he could.

CONTINUED

75 CONTINUED

> ANATOLE
> I think he can and will. He,
> just tonight spoke of such things.
> Things will look brighter after a
> good night's rest.

During this speech, Anatole has lighted a candle taken from the mantel and as he ends it he starts for the stairway followed by Talbot.

76 INT. YVONNE'S BEDROOM - MED - NIGHT

It is a small, character room such as might be found in a story-and-a-half house. The walls are roughly plastered giving it a rather monastic atmosphere which is relieved by a portion of the ceiling which slants to conform with the slope of the roof. Outside the pair of small-paned casement windows the night id dark. The room is furnished sparsely and in keeping with the modest circumstances of the home. A rather high, old fashioned bed is covered with a hand-made patchwork spread. Besides this there are a couple of straight-backed chairs and a chest of drawers above which is hung a dark-framed mirror.

Yvonne, clad in a simple, high-necked, but not too dowdy night gown, sits on the edge of the bed looking at the rope of pearls in her hands. She holds them off at arm's length. Now she rises and crossing quickly to the mirror, she sizes up the effect then slips them over her head in a double loop and studies the effect in the glass.

77 INT. YVONNE'S BEDROOM - MED. CLOSE - NIGHT

on Yvonne at mirror. The CAMERA ANGLE shows both the girl and her reflection in the mirror. The angle of incidence is such that the mirror also shows the reflection of the room's single door that leads out into the upper corridor. Yvonne sizes up her appearance in the mirror and shifts the string of pearls about appraisingly. In doing so she becomes conscious of the thin chain and crucifix. Recalling what Count Dracula told her about its spoiling the effect, she lifts it in her fingers thoughtfully, then hides the cross in her hand as best she can to see how it works. Now growing more curious, she unfastens the thin chain and removing it, she regards the effect appraisingly. As she does so, the door (as reflected in the mirror) is seen to open slowly. She freezes into immobility staring at it. It swings wide open. There is no one in the doorway. She turns quickly and looks at it. CAMERA SWINGS TO THE DOOR and (TRICK SHOT) discloses Count Dracula in the doorway. He bows rather stiffly and with out taking his eyes off the girl o.s.

> DRACULA
> They are beautiful as I told you,
> are they not?

CONTINUED

77   CONTINUED
Still holding the girl's eyes with his, he moves slowly toward her.

78   INT. YVONNE'S BEDROOM - MED. - NIGHT
on Yvonne at mirror. She is staring PAST CAMERA at the advancing Count. Now she starts backing away. The Count enters from CAMERA following her slowly. The room is not large and she eventually comes up against the wall. She starts uncoiling the pearls from her throat and as the Count gets within arm's length of her, she throws one arm across her eyes and holds out the beads toward him as she says:

                    YVONNE
            Here! Take them!

CAMERA HAS FOLLOWED IN CLOSE with the two and is now shooting over the Count's shoulder full on Yvonne. The hand with which she thrusts out the pearls also holds the slender chain and crucifix. The action is unintentional, but God is apparently with her, for as she holds out the jewels, she frees the crucifix and it hangs dangling before the Count's eyes. He shrinks back, covers his eyes with a spasmodic gesture and draws back out of the scene. After a moment, Yvonne uncovers her eyes to see why he has not taken the jewels. He is gone. She looks toward the door.

79   INT. YVONNE'S BEDROOM - MED. - NIGHT

SHOOTING TOWARD the corridor door. It stands open. No one is in sight. Yvonne enters from camera and goes thru the door to the corridor to see what has become of the Count. She looks first toward the rear of the corridor, then down the stairs to the kitchen.

80   INT. KITCHEN - MED. ON STAIR LANDING - NIGHT (TRICK SHOT)

The room is lighted only by the flickering of the fire in the o.s. fireplace. From under the closed stairway door a thin, shimmering vapor is oozing and drifting off toward the window on the far side of the room.

jm

81   INT KITCHEN - MED. AT WINDOW - NIGHT - (TRICK SHOT)

The wisp of vapor is floating in from the direction of the stairway and narrowing into a ribbon to disappear thru the crack under the window sash. As the last of it disappears thru the crack, a huge bat flaps its way up from below the window ledge outside the window. It hovers a moment, looking in thru the glass, then turns and wings its way off into the night.

DISSOLVE TO

82   LONG SHOT - NIGHT - (STOCK)

Miniature of castle in "Frankenstein Meets the Wolfman".

DISSOLVE TO

83   EXT. CASTLE GATES FROM MOAT - NIGHT
(Tower of London Set)
Low camera set-up in moat with drawbridge and heavy gates hanging askew, upstage. The moat is strewn with massive blocks of masonry that have fallen from the walls. Growing crooked from the ruins are dead-limbed trees. The huge bat flies in from camera to the drawbridge and disappears through the sagging gates.

84   EXT. CASTLE COURTYARD - FULL TOWER OF LONDON SET

This is not a courtyard in the generally accepted sense of the term, but is instead a private graveyard, the headstones fallen, or tilted drunkenly and too badly eroded by time and the elements for the inscriptions to be legible. Leafless trees thrust their naked branches up from the stony soil and an accumulation of dead tumble weeds which have blown into the corners in drifts. A door of the castle stands open. The bat flies through the scene from the gates to the open door and as it disappears through it, the door swings shut slowly with a dismal creaking.

85   INT. FIRST CASTLE CORRIDOR - FULL ("GREEN HELL" SET)

Bat flies from camera to upstage door standing ajar and again as it passes through the door swings shut behind it.

DISSOLVE TO

86   INT. SECOND CASTLE CORRIDOR - FULL
It is full of fallen masonry - a picture of dilapidation and ruin. The bat flies the length of the corridor and disappears behind a pile of fallen masonry at the far end.

87   int. stair tower - ("green hell" set)

Bat flies in through upper door, dives down, following the course of the circular stairs and out of scene.

88   INT. CRYPT - FULL

It is a huge chamber and practically empty. At the extreme end is a raised platform set within a sort of alcove, the crumbling upper portion of which is supported by a couple of crumbling pillars. On the platform are two heavy coffins, one open, the other closed. The bat flies in from camera and straight to the platform where it comes to a stop and transforms into Dracula. The platform is lighted by a faint fan of night light that falls slant-wise upon it from some break or window in the wall o.s.

89   INT. CRYPT - NIGHT - MED. CLOSE

on Dracula on the platform. He glances off in the direction of the light source, then moves towards the coffin. CAMERA DOLLIES A FEW FEET with him, till it brings into scene behind him the upper edge of the lid of his coffin, then lets Dracula go on out of scene and holds on coffin lid. After a second's interval, the lid is seen to start to close. CAMERA PANS with it as it is nearly shut and shows Dracula's fingers thrust out through the crack, as the lid is lowered the last couple of inches

90   STOCK SHOT OF SUNRISE
as the sun just starts to peep up over the horizon.

                                          FADE OUT

FADE IN

91 INT. KITCHEN - MED. AT STAIR LANDING - DAY
    The door is opening from the other side. Talbot backs
    INTO SCENE quietly, carrying his shoes and obviously
    intent upon disturbing no one. He closes the door
    cautiously and turns to go on down the stairs. He stops
    short at sight of someone in the room below him. As he
    stares, CAMERA PULLS QUICKLY BACK to disclose Yvonne
    seated on a bench at the big table writing rapidly. Her
    back is to the stairs and she is not aware of Talbot's
    entrance. As he starts on down the steps, she finishes
    her note and rising, takes the rope of pearls from her
    pocket and lays them on it. Then she takes up a shawl-
    wrapped bundle from the bench beside her and starts for
    the door to the compound. At sight of Talbot she stops
    short in surprise.

                    TALBOT
                (casually)
            Good morning.

Then as he makes his way to a chair and sits to pull on
his shoes he continues speaking.

                    TALBOT
            I wonder which of us is more
            surprised.

The girl doesn't answer.

                    TALBOT
            Why are you running away?

                    YVONNE
            Why do you think I'm running away?
                    TALBOT
            It's rather obvious - that bundle
            in your hand and the note on the table.

She still says nothing. He finishes fastening his shoes
and rising crosses to take up his hat from where he left
it the night before.

                    TALBOT
                (crossing)
            You needn't be afraid to talk.
            I'm leaving, too.

                    YVONNE
            Why?
                    TALBOT
            Your father wants to send
            me to Count Dracula. That old crow!
            He couldn't help me if he would; and he
            wouldn't help me if he could!

                                        CONTINUED

91 CONTINUED

>   YVONNE
>   My father had agreed to let
>   him marry me.

>   TALBOT
>   What!

>   YVONNE
>   (indicating pearls)
>   There's his engagement present.

>   TALBOT
>   (admiring it)
>   That's quite a bribe to give up.

>   YVONNE
>   Not if I have to take the Count
>   with it.

>   TALBOT
>   We seem to think a good deal alike.
>   Here - let me carry that for you.

He takes the bundle from her hand and they head for the door.

(CLOSE UPS TO COVER ABOVE)

92 INT. KITCHEN - MED. - DAY

As Talbot and Yvonne EXIT through the door the CAMERA SWINGS to the stairway and shows Anatole coming through the stairway door just in time to miss seeing the other two. He comes quickly down the steps and starts for the fireplace to rebuild the fire, but stops short at sight of the note on the table. He takes it up in surprise to read it.

93 EXT. COMPOUND NEAR GATEWAY - DAY

CAMERA IS DOLLYING ahead of Talbot and Yvonne on their was to the compound gateway.

>   TALBOT
>   Have you made any definite plans?

>   YVONNE
>   (tonelessly)
>   I'll go into service somewhere.
>   What else can I do?

CONTINUED

93   CONTINUED

                    TALBOT
                (cheerfully)
            Why not marry some young fellow
            in Slavno?

                    YVONNE
            Even in Slavno they point me out
            as the hangman's daughter.

As she finishes the line, they are rounding the corner
of the gateway. Talbot draws the girl quickly out of
sight as they hear Anatole calling o.c.

                    ANATOLE'S VOICE
                (o.s.
            Yvonne! Yvonne!

94   EXT. ANATOLE'S COTTAGE - MED. - FULL - DAY

The door is open and Anatole stands outside, the note
clutched in one hand. He has evidently just come outside, but apparently has failed to see the two runaways.
He hurries to the compound wall to look down the road.
He turns back slowly, unhappily - looks down at the note
and moves listlessly back toward the house.

95   EXT. COMPOUND - MED. AT WALL OUTSIDE GATE - DAY

Talbot and Yvonne disc. where we last saw them, their
attention on Anatole back by the house. The girl steals
a look around the corner and turns back rather gloomily.
Talbot, watching her, guesses what is in her mind.

                    TALBOT
            You don't really want to leave
            your father, do you?

                    YVONNE
                (shaking her head)
            It's going to be awfully lonely
            for him here - by himself.

Together they start forward, CAMERA DOLLYING WITH THEM

                    TALBOT
            If there was only some way to get
            rid of our friend the Count, you'd - -

He stops short as an idea strikes him.

                    YVONNE
            What is it?   CONTINUED

95 CONTINUED

                    TALBOT
          Oh, on idea just occurred to
          me...

He laughs it off rather sell-consciously and CAMERA
PANS with them.

                    YVONNE
          What sort of idea?

                    TALBOT
          Oh, just a wild one - too crazy
          even to talk about.

He ends the line as they are walking down the hill road
stretching away from CAMERA.

                                                FADE OUT

FADE IN

96 INT. KITCHEN - NIGHT

It is approximately the set-up we had when we first saw
the room the previous night. Anatole stands as before
at the window looking out into the compound, as if hoping
for the return of Yvonne. From o.s. comes the voice of
Count Dracula.

                    DRACULA'S VOICE
                      (o.s.)
          You say she has never done a
          thing like this before?

                    ANATOLE
          Never.

He turns from the window to move upstage to the fireplace
CAMERA PANNING to show the Count leaning against a corner
of the chimney, dour, sinister, his face in shadow as he
watches Anatole. CAMERA DOLLIES WITH Anatole and ends
on a MED SHOT of the two men. As Anatole approaches, the
Count speaks, but remains motionless, only his eyes
following Anatole.

                    DRACULA
          And you're quite sure she left no
          word of explanation - no note?

                    ANATOLE
              (dissembling)
          She - she left your engagement
          gift as I told you   CONTINUED

96 CONTINUED

The Count lifts a hand and looks down at the rope of pearls held loosely in his fingers.

> DRACULA
> The implication in that
> seems fairly obvious.

CAMERA DOLLIES IN CLOSE on the Count as he raises his eyes and fixes them coldly on Anatole.

> DRACULA
> I am not altogether pleased with
> you Anatole. You promised I
> should marry Yvonne.

97 INT. KITCHEN - CLOSE - NIGHT
on Anatole. He lowers his eyes from the Count's and stares into the fire as he protests.

> ANATOLE
> I could hardly force such a
> wedding if she were unwilling.

The Count's hand, with the pearls still twined through the fingers stabs into the scene and clutches Anatole by the slack of his shirtfront, CAMERA DOLLYING BACK to INCLUDE the doctor as he holds the other, staring coldly into his eyes.

> DRACULA
> I'm holding you to your promise!
> Wherever she is, I want he found
> and brought back!

For a moment he holds Anatole thus, helpless. Then their attention is attracted to a SOUND at the door o.s. and he loosens his grip as both look toward the SOUND.

98 INT. KITCHEN - MED. AT DOOR TO COMPOUND - NIGHT
The door opens and Talbot steps inside. In one hand he carries Yvonne's shawl-wrapped bundle, with a smaller one wrapped in paper under his arm

> TALBOT
> Good evening, Anatole, Count Dracula.

CONTINUED

98 CONTINUED
As he speaks the girl ENTERS, the same drab, uninteresting peasant girl - perhaps even a trifle more mouse-like from her reluctance to face the scene that she suspects will follow. Talbot pushes the door closed, and taking the girl's hand leads her across to the stairway. CAMERA DOLLIES AND PANS with them to hold in the background Anatole who moves forward to intercept them at the foot of the steps.

                    ANATOLE
                   (crossing)
            Yvonne! What does this mean?
            Where have you been?

He reaches them at the foot of the stairs as the girl is starting up. She stops. It is Talbot who answers.

                    TALBOT
                   (to Yvonne)
            Run along to your room and put on
            the little present I bought you.

As he speaks he is handing her the two bundles which she takes awkwardly as she protests:

                    YVONNE
            But I -

                    TALBOT
                   (interrupting quickly)
            It'll be best to let me explain.

The girl hesitates, looks at her father, then really glad of a chance to escape a scene, she hurries up the steps. During this Anatole has stood watching, stern-eyed and silent. The Count has remained where he was, at the corner of the fireplace. As the girl disappears through the door, Anatole turns to Talbot.

99 INT. KITCHEN - CLOSE AT FOOT OF STAIRS - NIGHT
Anatole turns from the girl to Talbot.

                    ANATOLE
            Well?

Talbot smiles unconcernedly

                    TALBOT
            The explanation's quite simple,
            really.

                                            CONTINUED

99 CONTINUED

As he speaks he passes Anatole on his way to the fireplace, the older man following and CAMERA DOLLYING WITH THEM.

          TALBOT
          (cont'd)
  Yvonne and I were married
  this afternoon in Slavno.

As he is finishing the line he has reached the fireplace and is spreading his hands before the comforting blaze. The Count stiffens perceptible. Anatole stops stock still as if frozen for a second. Then:

          ANATOLE
       (slowly - incredulously)
  You - married - my daughter?

          TALBOT
       (warming his hands)
  Why not?

          ANATOLE
        (outraged)
WHY NOT!

He lays a hand on Talbot's shoulder and spins him round to face him.

          ANATOLE
         (cont'd)
  After what you told me about
  yourself last night?

100 INT. KITCHEN - CLOSE TWO SHOT - NIGHT

Anatole is glaring furiously at Talbot who smiles at him and replies mockingly.

          TALBOT
  Oh, but you don't believe all that
  nonsense, Anatole! There's not such
  thing as a werewolf! You said so
  yourself! Surely you haven't changed
  your mind overnight!

Anatole is caught in a split stick and knows it, but tries to save face.

          ANATOLE
       (unconvincingly)
  No, of course not, but - you
  can't be in love with her! You
  hardly know her.

CONTINUED

100 CONTINUED

> TALBOT
> (smiling craftily)
> Has it occurred to you that I may have married her - because you love her?

> ANATOLE
> I don't understand.

> TALBOT
> Are you so sure of your opinions that you dare trust your daughter to my keeping? Do you dare risk what will happen at the next full moon, if I turn into - -

> ANATOLE
> (interrupting)
> Stop! You have no right to - -

> TALBOT
> (continuing impassibly)
> Or will you make a silver bullet and do what I asked you to?

> ANATOLE
>
> No, I will not! You have no right to ask me to do murder!

CAMERA DRAWS BACK as Anatole drops miserably into a chair. Talbot stares down at him importantly.

> TALBOT
> You are a fool!

Then he smiles slowly and continues:

> TALBOT
> But perhaps you'll change your mind before the next full moon.

Turning back to the fire, he glances at the Count who has stood by, a silent, sinister witness to the scene. As if aware of him for the first time, Talbot address him.

> TALBOT
> (insincerely)
> I'm sorry to have upset your plans for the girl, Count

101 INT. KITCHEN - CLOSE - NIGHT
on the Count. His eyes are fixed venomously on Talbot o.s.

                    DRACULA
            My plans remain the same - - and
            it is you who are the fool! You
            dug a pit for Anatole - it is you
            who will fall into it!

102 INT. KITCHEN - MED. - NIGHT
on Talbot and the Count. Talbot glances at the other over his shoulder and says unconcernedly.

                    TALBOT
            Is that a prediction - or a threat?

                    DRACULA
            Both. I see a bit further than
            most men. At present you want
            to die, but before the next full
            moon, you'll pray for life, so
            you can keep what you have taken.
            Look!

He points off PAST CAMERA in the direction of the stair landing. Talbot turns casually to see. The cynical smile fades from his lips as he stares incredulously at what he sees and he half whispers the one word:

                    TALBOT
            Yvonne!

103 INT. KITCHEN - MED. FULL - NIGHT

on stairway from Talbot's angle. Yvonne is coming through the door to the landing, but she is no longer the drab, uninteresting little peasant girl we have known. The coarse, gray, unbecoming dress is gone and in its place she wears a white one, trimmed gaily with bright colors. The clumsy slate colored kerchief is gone from her head, allowing her soft blond hair to fall to her shoulders. But more even than this, her expression has changed from its former dead, hopelessness. The girl glows with a new radiance as she ENTERS half timidly to the stair rail and smiles down at Talbot o.s. Smoothing the gathers of the skirt she asks naively:

                                        CONTINUED

103   CONTINUED

                    YVONNE
           DO- do you like me in it?

Talbot ENTERS silently, his eyes fixed on the girl he
has so unsuspectingly married.

104   INT. KITCHEN - CLOSE - NIGHT
       on the Count. He looks after Talbot with a thin smile.

                    DRACULA
           Don't forget - it is only three
           weeks till the next full moon.

He bows slightly and moves toward the door.

                                                FADE OUT

       FADE IN

105   EXT. DIRT ROAD THROUGH HILLS - FULL - DAY
       Set up is chosen for scenic beauty - rolling hills and
       oaks. MOVING TOWARD CAMERA is a rick piled high with
       hay, drawn by a span of heavy draft horses. Talbot is
       driving and Yvonne is on the lead with him although it
       is too far away to recognize them. As the team plods
       up the slight incline, the girl's VOICE is HEARD sing-
       ing a merrily little fold song (Hungarian or Austrian).

                                                DISSOLVE TO

106   EXT. ROAD - CLOSE (PROCESS) - DAY

       on Yvonne, dressed in a becoming peasant dress. She is
       half lying back against the hay, her hands clasped un-
       der her head, eyes on the sky above and singing the
       song first heard in previous scene. As she sings, the
       CAMERA DOLLIES BACK to include Talbot. He is sitting
       slightly forward of her position to handle the horses
       and seems rather moody. She finishes the song, and
       removing her hands from under her head holds them
       above her face and starts counting on her fingers.
       Then she sits up suddenly wide-eyed.

                    YVONNE
           Larry!

                                                CONTINUED

106 CONTINUED
He snaps out of his reverie and turns to her with a little smile and says:

      TALBOT
  Yes?

      YVONNE
  Do you know what day this is?

      TALBOT
    (studying)
  I don't think I do. I know last
  night was the dark of the moon.

yvonne hitches herself up beside him and slips an arm through his.

      YVONNE
  It's our wedding anniversary!

      TALBOT
  Our anniversary!

      YVONNE
  Of course! We've been married a
  week today.

He lays his hand over hers with a wry smile.

      TALBOT
  One week gone out of three.

He turns away from her and looks ahead along the road. She regards him curiously, then:

      YVONNE
  What's troubling you, Larry?
  Aren't you happy?

      TALBOT
    (solemnly)
  I've never been so happy in my
  life - nor so miserable.

She studies him, puzzled, for a moment, then smiles and nestles closer.

      YVONNE
  You mustn't be afraid that stupid
  old Count's prediction will come
  true.

          CONTINUED

106   CONTINUED - 2

                    TALBOT
          I think I'm even more afraid it
          won't.

The smile fades from Yvonne's lips and she draws away
from him, looking at him with real hurt in her eyes.
Talbot doesn't notice, but raising his hand, waves to
someone o.s. ahead of the wagon.

107   EXT. GATEWAY TO COMPOUND - FULL - DAY

SHOOTING THROUGH the gateway toward the cottage. The
hayrick is driving through the gate. Anatole is seen
near the cottage. He waves back and strolls down to
meet the wagon. Talbot brings it to a stop some distance from him, and leaping to the ground puts his arms
up to help Yvonne down.

108   EXT. COMPOUND - MED. - DAY
at wagon as Yvonne leans forward, puts her hands on
Talbot's shoulders and lets him lift her to the ground.
As she lands on her feet, she leaves her hands about
his neck and watching him searchingly, asks soberly:

                    YVONNE
          You didn't mean what you just
          said, did you, Larry?

                    TALBOT
          I don't know what I mean. I'm all
          mixed up. I only know that I --

He stops short and both look toward the gateway o.s. as
they hear the SOUND of approaching HOOFS at a trot.

109   EXT. COMPOUND - MED. FULL - DAY

Talbot and Yvonne in f.g. looking toward the gateway
through which is riding a peasant on a work horse. He
carries a rusty old single barreled shotgun across his
saddle. Anatole ENTERS from CAMERA as the rider reins
up facing the group.

                    HORSEMAN
          Good morning, Anatole. Have you seen
          any wolf tracks around here in the
          last couple of days?

anatole has crossed to him during the speech.

am 57

110 EXT. COMPOUND - MED. - DAY
on Anatole and horseman.

                    ANATOLE
          A wolf? Are you joking. There
          hasn't been a wolf in those hills
          in the past hundred years.

                    HORSEMAN
          There was last night. He killed
          Emil Vardek's wife. Tore her
          throat so she bled to death.

111 EXT. COMPOUND - MED. - DAY
on Talbot and Yvonne listening to the story, The girl's
eyes widen with horror and she draws closer to Talbot.

112 EXT. COMPOUND - MED. - DAY

on Anatole and horseman.

                    ANATOLE
          It couldn't have been a wolf.

                    HORSEMAN
          It was, by the tracks - - - a huge
          one. And they led in this direction.

                    ANATOLE
          Won't you get down and -

                    HORSEMAN
               (interrupting)
          Thanks - I want to warn the other
          farmers. Keep a gun handy and
          watch your stock.

As he is finishing he reins his horse around and with a
wave of the hand heads out through the gate at a trot.
Anatole turns and moves toward Talbot and Yvonne -
thoughtfully. CAMERA PANS HIM to them.

                    ANATOLE
          Run along and set the table, Yvonne
          while we put away the team.

The girl EXITS. Talbot turns to the team and throws off
the horse's rein across to the far side. As he moves to
unfasten a trace, Anatole follows and stops behind him

                                              CONTINUED

112 CONTINUED

> ANATOLE
> That's a terrible thing Hans just told us.

> TALBOT
> Horrible.

113 EXT. COMPOUND - MED. - DAY
on Anatole and Talbot. Anatole watches the other closely to see the effect of his next line.

> ANATOLE
> Especially since there are no ordinary wolves in these hills.

It takes Talbot a split second to catch the implication in the line. Then he turns and peers into Anatole's face to be sure is not mistaken.

> TALBOT
> You mean you think that I --

> ANATOLE
> (interrupting)
> I only know what you told me about yourself - and last night was a change of the moon.

For a second Talbot remains silent, grave - then with a sardonic smile about his lips he shakes his head and replies:

> TALBOT
> No change of the moon affects me, Anatole - till it turns full. Then be ready with the silver bullet.

He stoops, and taking up the loose rein starts looping it to hang it on the hames as if the matter is ended.

> ANATOLE
> (desperately)
> But why must I do it? Why not do it yourself?

> TALBOT
> Because I can only be killed while I am the beast - and then I don't want to die!

FADE OUT

es

114 INSERT - CLOSE UP
on Bohemian calendar for the month of September.
CAMERA DOLLIES IN to CLOSE UP on the date that is
marked with the change of the moon to the first
quarter. OVER THE SCENE we hear Yvonne's VOICE
quietly, but happily, singing the same little
folk song she was singing on the hayrick.

                DISSOLVE TO

115 INT. KITCHEN - MED. FULL - NIGHT
at fireplace at an angle that includes the kitchen
alcove upstage. Yvonne is disc. at the work table
as she was seen earlier, straining milk from the
wooden bucket into the shallow pans. Her father is
looking at the calendar on the wall; he turns away
from it and quizzically looks at the girl as the
song ends.

      ANATOLE
   Have you really been as happy
   the past two weeks as you have
   seemed, Yvonne?

She turns to him with eyes glowing.

      YVONNE
   Happy? Even if it should end
   tomorrow, I could live the rest
   of my life on the memory of it.

Anatole turns to knock the ashes from his pipe as he
answers gravely.

      ANATOLE
   Well, we'll know in another week
   how it will end.

Yvonne, who has returned to her work, turns and looks
at him in quick surprise.

      YVONNE
   Why in another week?

      ANATOLE
   That's the next full moon.

The girl regards him curiously, then moves downstage to
him, speaking as she approaches.

                CONTINUED

115 CONTINUED

> YVONNE
> The next full moon! I don't think I understand.

It is now Anatole's turn to show his bewilderment as he searches the girl's face.

> ANATOLE
> You mean you don't know why Larry came here in the first place?

> YVONNE
> (shaking her head)
> No — was there some special reason?

Anatole turns away to fireplace, realizing he has got himself in an embarrassing spot and hunting a way out.

> ANATOLE
> I'm sorry. I wouldn't have mentioned it, but I thought of course he'd told you.

> YVONNE
> (lightly)
> Well, he hasn't. What was the reason?

> ANATOLE
> (uncomfortably)
> I shouldn't have mentioned it. It's really his secret.

> YVONNE
> (banteringly)
> Oh, but you've said too much to stop now. Why did he come here?

Seeing that he can't escape without getting tough, Anatole faces her.

> anatole
> He came to me because I'm the hangman - and he wanted to die.

The smile fades from the girl's lips and she stares at him incredulously. When she speaks the words are barely audible.

> YVONNE
> Oh, no - he couldn't have! Why would he want to die?

> ANATOLE
> That's a question I have no right to answer.

CONTINUED

115 CONTINUED - 2

                    YVONNE
          Then I'll get it from him!
          Where is he?

                    ANATOLE
          Believe me, my dear, it's best
          to let the matter drop.

                    YVONNE
          How can I? I know too much, or
          too little! Where is he?

                    ANATOLE
              (helplessly)
          He went down the trail toward
          the Volchek farm.

Yvonne snatches up a light shawl and runs out the door drawing the shawl about her shoulders. Anatole turns away unable to make up his mind what he ought to do. Moving to the fireplace he starts to bring an old muzzle-loader from where it stands in the corner, hesitates, then leans it back in place, still unwilling to concede to Talbot's wishes.
(CLOSE-UPS TO BREAK UP ABOVE)

116 EXT. COMPOUND - AT GATEWAY - NIGHT - (TRICK SHOT)

Upstage the windows of the cottage are lighted. Yvonne is discovered hurrying toward camera at half-run. She EXITS past it and as she does the sinister figure of Count Dracula emerges from the shadows a short distance inside the compound and for a moment looks after her. Then he lifts his arms out straight from his shoulders, the cape of his great coat draping like huge wings. Suddenly they turn into wings - bat-wings; the Count has disappeared, changed into a bat which flies down to camera and hovers before it looking out in the direction Yvonne went. After a moment it flaps off after her.

117 EXT. COMPOUND - SHOOTING AWAY FROM IT - NIGHT

Yvonne ENTERS from camera, hurries to a point where a path breaks down over the edge of the hill and stops, looking down into the canyon.
                    YVONNE
              (Calling)
          Larry!
Getting no answer she hurries down the trail and out of sight. As she disappears below the break in the ground, the bat flaps in from camera and swoops down over the edge of the hill on the same course taken by the girl.

                                        DISSOLVE

118 EXT TRAIL - MED. - NIGHT

Talbot disc. seated dejectedly on a fallen tree near a small grove or heavy growth of brush, striving vainly to solve the problem he knows is hopeless. He lifts his head from his cupped hands and raises his eyes to the heavens - in a half-playful attitude.

119 STOCK SHOT OF NEW MOON THRU CLOUDS

120 EXT. TRAIL - MED. - NIGHT

Talbot closes his eyes and rising wearily from the log, starts back along the trail toward Anatole's

121 EXT. TRAIL - MED. FULL - NIGHT

Yvonne comes round a bend in the trail and hurries down it TOWARD CAMERA. As she reaches a moonlit spot in middle foreground, she stops short, her attention caught by something coming toward her along trail beyond camera.

122 EXT. TRAIL - FULL - NIGHT

from Yvonne's angle. A man disc. coming up the trail TOWARD CAMERA. He is near enough in size and dress to be Larry.

123 EXT. TRAIL - MED. CLOSE - NIGHT

on Yvonne. Her eyes light up as she thinks she sees Larry. She half runs from scene to meet him. As she hurries out, CAMERA PANS A FEW STEPS WITH HER. THEN BACK to show the bat flap INTO SCENE. It comes into f.g., where it hangs in midair flapping its wings before darting out along the trail in the direction taken by Yvonne.

124 EXT. TRAIL - MED FULL - NIGHT

PAN WITH YVONNE as she runs TOWARD CAMERA and toward the man o.s. who is approaching from opposite direction. As she nears him she stops short, realizing it is not her husband, as she had thought. The man is Geza Volcheck and now that we are closer to him we see that he has an old single-barreled shotgun held in the crook of his arm. He approaches her, touching his cap, as he says

      GEZA
    Good Evening, Yvonne   CONTINUED

124 CONTINUED

                    YVONNE
                      (disappointed)
                Good evening, Geza. For a moment
                I thought you were my husband.
                Have you seen him?

125 EXT. TRAIL - MED. - NIGHT

                    GIZA
                Yes, I passed him further down
                the path, but - -

                    YVONNE
                      (interrupting)
                Thank you.

She starts to hurry past him, but he stops her.

                    GEZA
                But I can't let you go to him.
                Those are orders.

                    YVONNE
                Orders! From whom?

                    GEZA
                From the Wolf Patrol. No woman or
                child is allowed alone in the hills
                at night.

He tries to start her back up the trail

                    YVONNE
                      (protesting)
                But I've got to see him! It's
                important!

                    GEZA
                      (gently)
                Whatever it is, it will keep. Come
                on - I'll see you safely home.

Unwillingly the girl lets him take her arm and start her back along the trail. CAMERA PANS THEM A FEW PACES on their way, THEN WHIPS BACK to see the bat again fly in from o.s., hover a moment in f.g., then dart away toward the hills at an angle but in the general direction the two have gone,

126 EXT. BRUSHY HILL - MED. FULL - NIGHT - (TRICK SHOT)
Bat flies in from camera and upstage toward the deep
shadows of a clump of oaks. As it reaches the shadows,
it turns into Dracula with cape spread like wings.
He turns to camera and looks off in the direction
from which he came.

127 EXT. HILLSIDE NEAR TREES - MED. CLOSE - NIGHT
on the doctor. He is looking out past camera at Yvonne
and Geza. Now he backs deeper into the shadows, then
turns and walks out of sight behind a small clump of
brush. The CAMERA PANS AT A WALKING GAIT to the far
side of the brush. But instead of Dracula coming
out, it is a wolf that slinks into view. A few feet
from the brush, it stops and looks back toward Yvonne
and Geza o.s.

128 EXT. HILL PATH - MED. FULL - NIGHT
from angle of the wolf. Yvonne and Geza seen moving
along the path.

129 EXT. HILL AT CLUMP OF BRUSH - MED. - NIGHT
on wolf looking off at Yvonne and Geza. Now he turns
his head and trots off at an angle as if to intercept
them farther along the trail.

130 EXT. AT PATH - MED FULL - NIGHT
at a cut bank. The wolf ENTERS through the brush on
the hillside and moves down to the edge of the path
where he stops and, keeping partly under cover, peers
down the path toward Yvonne and Geza. Now he turns
and starts up the slope to the top of the cut bank
overlooking the trail.

131 EXT. PATH - FULL - NIGHT
from top of cut bank. Over the edge of bank in f.g.,
Yvonne and Geza are seen approaching along the path
unaware of any danger. The wolf slinks INTO SCENE
moves to the edge of the bank and crouches down ready
to spring when the two victims pass under him.

132 EXT. PATH - CLOSE - NIGHT
at top of cut bank. The wolf crawls forward thru the high grass, eyes on the two victims approaching below him. Now he crouches in position for the spring and then leaps down and OUT PAST CAMERA.

133 EXT. PATH - MED. - NIGHT
Yvonne and Geza approaching camera. As they come into immediate f.g., and girl looks up, screams and leaps back. Gesa looks up too late. The wolf leaps in from above full on him and bears him backward from the scene before he has a chance to get the gun up for a shot.

134 EXT. PATH - MED. - NIGHT
Yvonne staggers back out of the way as the wolf's leap carries Gesa to the ground, the gun flying out of his hands. The wolf goes for the man's throat, breaking through his frantic efforts to ward it off.

135 EXT. PATH - CLOSE - NIGHT
on Yvonne as she watches, horrified. Her eyes turn from the struggling man to the spot where the gun fell and she runs out toward it.

136 EXT. PATH - MED. - NIGHT
Geza struggling with the wolf as Yvonne runs in and snatches up the fallen gun. She struggles to get it cocked.

137 EXT. PATH - CLOSE - NIGHT
Yvonne gets gun cocked and, raising it rather clumsily to her shoulder, aims it at the wolf o.s. and fires

138 EXT. PATH - MED - NIGHT

The wolf is still on the man and is worrying at his throat. There is smoke in the air from the discharged gun, but the wolf pays no attention to it. At such close range it is obvious that the girl couldn't have missed. She backs off nonplussed at the failure of the shot to have stopped the wolf. The gun falls from her hands and she turns and runs down the path toward where we last saw Larry.

139 EXT. PATH - MED. FULL - NIGHT
Larry disc. coming up the path, listlessly. Suddenly, from a distance ahead, he hears Yvonne's VOICE o.s. calling:

>   YVONNE'S VOICE
>   Larry! Larry!

Alarmed by the girl's tone, he stops short; then, breaking into a run, he hurries out past camera in the direction from which the voice came.

140 EXT. PATH - MED. FULL - NIGHT
SHOOTING UP THE PATH. Yvonne runs in from around a bend in the trail. Apparently she sees Larry coming, for again she calls his name - this time in relief. CAMERA PANS her as she stumbles out past it and we see her reach the approaching Larry and fall into his arms, clinging to him.

141 EXT. PATH - CLOSER - NIGHT
Yvonne stumbles into Larry's arms sobbing hysterically.

>   TALBOT
>   Yvonne! What is it?
>
>   YVONNE
>   (between sobs)
>   The wolf! It's killing Geza
>   Volchek! Hurry!

Talbot steadies the girl a second, then runs back along the path to help Volchek. Yvonne hurries after him as best she can.

142 EXT. PATH - MED - NIGHT
At scene of attack. In their struggles, the wolf and Geza have worked their way to the edge of the path where woods and tall grass hide the man's head and the upper part of his body, at which the wolf has been tearing. The wolf itself stands over him, head down. Almost immediately the head comes up and he stares down the trail in the direction from which Talbot is approaching.

143 EXT. PATH - FULL - NIGHT

A flash of Talbot coming on the run as he rounds a bend in the path some little distance away.

144 EXT. PATH AT SCENE OF ATTACK - MED. - NIGHT
Wolf disc. standing over victim and looking off at
Talbot. He turns and casually trots off in the
direction from which he originally came. CAMERA PANNING
him till he disappears around edge of out bank.

145 EXT. HILLSIDE - MED. FULL - NIGHT
Wolf enters on a trot from camera, continues upstage
to a clump of brush where he stops and turns to look
back at the man lying on the path o.s.

146 EXT. PATH - AT SCENE OF ATTACK - MED. - NIGHT
The body of Geza lies at the edge of the grass as last
seen, arms outflung and motionless. Talbot hurries
INTO SCENE, takes a quick look off in the direction the
wolf went, then drops on one knee beside Geza to investigate his injuries.

147 EXT. HILLSIDE AT CLUMP OF BRUSH - MED. NIGHT
The wolf stands in the tall grass looking off at Talbot
and Geza. Now it turns and slinks into the brush. As
it is lost to sight, there is a moment's pause, then the
big bat flies out of the brush, rises about it and
hovers an instant looking off toward Talbot, then wheels
and flies off back toward Anatole's farmhouse.

148 EXT. PATH - MED. NIGHT

CAMERA is CUTTING ABOVE the body of the wolf's victim
as Talbot makes a cursory examination, his expression
showing his horror at the mangled throat. Yvonne is
hurrying towards him along the path. Talbot hears her
footsteps and rises to meet her before she can get a
look at the body. He stops her and she clings to him.

>   TALBOT
> Better not look, Yvonne. It's
> pretty ugly

For a moment they stand thus. Then:

>   TALBOT
> Show me the was to his farm. I'll
> have to take him there.

He turns away from her and stoops over the fallen man.
As he starts to lift him from the ground,

                                            DISSOLVE TO

149   INT. KITCHEN - MED. - NIGHT

   Dracula disc., seated with back to camera beside
   the table as when first we saw him. Anatole is moving
   nervously back and forth before the fireplace, apparently
   finishing a speech.

                    ANATOLE
            Of course in telling you the story,
            I've betrayed his confidence, but
            I had to go to someone for advice.

   He stops speaking and looks directly at Dracula
   waiting for a reply.

                    DRACULA
            From what you tell me, I'd say
            you have a madman for a son-in-
            law. A homicidal maniac.

                    ANATOLE
                      (sighing)
            I was afraid you'd say that. It
            leaves me no choice. I'll have to
            report him to the authorities.

150   INT KITCHEN - CLOSE - NIGHT
   on Dracula. He lifts his eyes thoughtfully at
   Anatole's remark and it is obvious that the idea does
   not fit in with some plan of his own. He sneaks a
   look at Anatole o.s.

                    DRACULA
            On the contrary. I may be able to
            help him. I have no great liking
            for the man, but it's my duty to
            cure him if I can.

   As he speaks he rises and moves to the fireplace beside
   Anatole. CAMERA FOLLOWING into a CLOSE SHOT favoring
   Anatole.

                    ANATOLE
                      (protestingly)
            But, that might take months!
            Meanwhile he'd be a constant
            menace to the countryside and to --

   He stops, and both turn their eyes toward the outer door
   as they HEAR the RATTLE of the latch.

bs   69

151   INT. KITCHEN - MED. FULL - NIGHT

       Camera includes the two men at the fireplace and the
       door to compound downstage. The door is opening.
       Talbot ENTERS, one arm about Yvonne who still shows
       effects of the experience she has just gone through.
       As he closes the door, Talbot speaks to Anatole.

                           TALBOT
                 Yvonne's just had a nasty shock.
                 She'd better go straight to her
                 room and rest.

       during the speech he has started across to the steps
       with her, CAMERA PANNING Anatole leaves his place
       at the fireplace and starts across to meet them at
       the foot of the steps. As he crosses he exclaims"

                           ANATOLE
                 What is it? What has happened?

       He reaches them in time to stop them as they start up
       the steps.

152   INT. KITCHEN - MED. NIGHT
       at foot of steps. Talbot and Yvonne come to a stop
       on about the second step and Talbot turns to answer
       Anatole.

                           TALBOT
                       (with uneasy look at girl)
                 A wolf just killed Geza Volchek.

       Anatole reacts. The girl adds:

                           YVONNE
                 I was with him when it attacked!

       Talbot starts on up with her. Anatole turns and looks
       off at the doctor.

153   INT. KITCHEN - CLOSE - NIGHT

       on Dracula as he intercepts Anatole's look and
       shakes his head dubiously.

154   INT. KITCHEN - MED. - NIGHT

       at foot of steps. Talbot has Yvonne at the door to
       the upper rooms. Anatole stops him from below.

                                                        CONTINUED

154 CONTINUED

                    ANATOLE
          If you can manage, my dear, I'd
          like to have a talk with Larry.

Talbot glances questioningly at the girl and starts to
protest. She gives him a faint smile.

                    YVONNE
          I'll be all right now.

She EXITS through the door. Talbot closes it, not too
sure he shouldn't go along. Then he starts down to
rejoin Anatole at the foot of the steps.

                    TALBOT
               (as he descends)
          What was it you wanted to know?

                    ANATOLE
          I was just wondering - were you
          with Yvonne when the wolf attacked?

                    TALBOT
          No, I was farther down the path at
          the time. Why do you ask?

During the speech he has reached Anatole and the two
have moved upstage to the fireplace, CAMERA FOLLOWING
THEM to end on a CLOSE THREE SHOT including the Count.

                    DRACULA
          What Anatole means is: Did the
          girl see you and the wolf - at
          the same time?

                    TALBOT
               (rather puzzled)
          No, I don't see how she could
          but - - -

He stops short as a possible significance to the
line strikes him.

155 INT. KITCHEN - CLOSE - NIGHT

on Talbot, as the full significance of the Count's
line strikes home. He looks from the doctor to Anatole
o.s. and a slow smile comes to his lips.

                    TALBOT
          Oh, I see what's in you mind!
          You think I killed Geza!

156	INT. KITCHEN - THREE SHOT - NIGHT
He finishes the line to Anatole who drops his eyes rather uncomfortably.

> ANATOLE
> (lamely)
> Well - tonight is another change of the moon.

> TALBOT
> I've told you a dozen times no change of the moon, except the full one turns me into a - -

He stops short as he realizes what he was about to say in the presence of a third party. He turns quickly to the Count and eyes him as he continues:

> TALBOT
> How much of my story has he told you?

> DRACULA
> Enough, so I'd like to convince you there's no such thing as a werewolf.

> TALBOT
> Why must all fools keep telling me that? Do you think I don't remember what I've done before - and know it will happen again?

Knowing the truth and knowing how hopeless it is to try to convince anyone else, he droops into a chair and buries his head in his hands, CAMERA MOVING BACK to FULLER SCENE.

> DRACULA
> I know you believe you remember. But there's a simple explanation of that. Did you ever hear of "lycanthropy"?

> TALBOT
> (not looking up)
> No.

> DRACULA
> It's a form of madness. Its victims honestly believe they turn to wild beasts in the full moon. It's the origin of all werewolf legends.

CONTINUED

156 CONTINUED

>   TALBOT
>   (hotly)
> I tell you it's not my imagination!
> I know! I've seen my victims!

>   DRACULA
> Even that is possible. The lycanthrope
> some times becomes violent - but he can
> still be cured.

Talbot rises wearily from the chair and leans an arm against the fireplace.

>   TALBOT
>   (hopelessly)
> Please - let's not argue! I'm
> afraid to go on living. It -
> it would be so much better to
> help me die!

He ends the line pleadingly to Anatole who lowers his eyes.

157 INT. KITCHEN - CLOSE - NIGHT
on Talbot with the Count behind him. The latter moves down closer and says quietly into his ear:

>   DOCTOR
>   (smiling)
> I don't think you really want
> to die!

Talbot turns his head quickly and looks at him hotly. The Count continues to smile thinly.

>   DOCTOR
> You've got too much to live
> for - now!

His eyes lift toward the upper rooms. Talbot gets the idea and his own eyes go up toward the upper rooms - and Yvonne. Still smiling, the doctor EXITS toward the door.

158 INT. KITCHEN - MED. NIGHT
at door. The Count ENTERS; he turns with one hand on the latch, and still smiling thinly says:

CONTINUED

158 CONTINUED
                        DRACULA
                Remember, I can cure you, my
                boy. All I ask in return is
                that you help with some - er
                work I have in mind.

He bows and EXITS.

                                                FADE OUT

     FADE IN

159 INT. KITCHEN - MED. FULL - DAY
     CAMERA SHOOTING TOWARD STAIRWAY. The door opens and
     Talbot comes in from upstairs. He glances toward the
     fireplace o.s., and seeing Anatole says:

                        TALBOT
                Good morning.

                        ANATOLE'S VOICE (O.S.)
                Good Morning.

Talbot has come downstairs and now CAMERA PANS with him
as he starts toward Anatole. The latter is rising from
a kneeling position before the fire with a crude iron
ladle in his hand. He approaches the end of the table
where the old rifle lies, powder horn beside it. On
the table beside it is a bullet mold. As the two men
approach one another Talbot says:

                        TALBOT
                You're up early.

                        ANATOLE
                Yes; I wanted to finish this
                before Yvonne comes down.

Anatole has reached the table and is pouring molten metal
into the bullet mold.

160 INT. KITCHEN - CLOSED - DAY

Anatole is pouring the metal into the mold as Talbot
ENTERS. The latter reacts to the collection of equip-
ment on the table. He seems not altogether too pleased.
Anatole turns the bullet mold over on the table.

161   INSERT - CLOSE
      as bullet mold is turned over and a shiny new bullet
      rolls out on the table.

162   INT. KITCHEN - MED. CLOSE - DAY
      on Anatole and Talbot looking down at the bullet. Talbot's
      eyes rise to the other's face. The significance of the
      silver bullet is not lost on him, but for some reason he
      doesn't seem as happy over it as might have been expected.

                    TALBOT
           Silver?
                    ANATOLE
               (nodding)
           Tomorrow's the full moon.

Talbot smiles thinly and there is a hint of sarcasm in
his tone as he replies:
                    TALBOT'
           So you finally believe what
           I've been telling you?

Anatole takes up the powder horn and starts pouring out
a charge in a small loader.

                    ANATOLE
           No - but I do intend to be
           prepared, in case I'm wrong.

He smiles wryly up at Talbot as he continues:

                    ANATOLE
           That ought to make you happy.

                    TALBOT
           Yes. I suppose it should - -

He turns away uneasily as he continues:

                    TALBOT
           But somehow, it doesn't.

Anatole stops in his business of loading the gun and
regards him in surprise.

                    ANATOLE
           I don't understand! You came to
           me half-crazed, begging me to - -
                    TALBOT
               (interrupting wearily)
           I know - I know! I came here begging you
           to help me die! - - - And now that you've
           agreed, I find that for the first time
           in my life - I want to live!

                                        CONTINUED

162 CONTINUED

His apathy drops from him and he turns almost frantically to the older man and says pleadingly:

      TALBOT
   I can't die, Anatole - not now!
   Don't you see I can't?

      ANATOLE
    (kindly)
   Are you afraid, son? -

Talbot slackens his grip on the other's arm and turns away.

      TALBOT
   No, no - it's not fear! It's -

He drops disconsolately to an end of the bench and with elbows on the table runs his fingers through his hair as he continues:

      TALBOT
   I never knew before that life could
   be anything but ugly! Now I know
   it can be beautiful!

As he ends the line, his eyes instinctively turn toward the stairs leading up to Yvonne. Anatole notices the look and glances up in the same direction as he gets the full import of Talbot's words.

      ANATOLE
    (gently)
   You mean Yvonne?
Talbot lowers his eyes, staring sightlessly at the table.

      TALBOT
    (dully)
   Yes, that's it - - Now that I've
   found her, I can't stand the
   thought of losing her.

He rises nervously, still keeping his eyes away as he continues:

      talbot
   I want to live, Anatole! I want
   to live - and have a home - just
   a small one - and -

He comes to a stop with a weary shake of the head. What words can he find to make his plight more clear? Anatole gives him a quizzical look.

      ANATOLE
   Didn't Count Dracula predict something
   like this?

          CONTINUED

162 CONTINUED - 2

> TALBOT
> Predict! That ghoul? Sometimes I feel as if he'd actually made it happen!

He turns and walks upstage, continuing his speech in a more normal tone.

> TALBOT
> That's absurd, of course.
>
> ANATOLE
> Of course. However, he was right.
>
> TALBOT
> (not turning)
> What if he was?

Anatole resumes the loading of the gun as he replies casually:

> ANATOLE
> If he was right in that, perhaps he was right in saying you're not what you believe - merely suffering from some form of hallucination.

Talbot's head come up slowly during the speech as he considers all its implications. At the end of it he turns quickly and regards the older man to see if he really means what he says. Then as he steps down to him he exclaims incredulously:

> TALBOT
> Do you really believe that?
>
> ANATOLE
> (imperturbably)
> My opinion doesn't matter. The Count is also a doctor - and he says he can cure you.

Talbot makes an exclamation of disgust and disbelief.

> ANATOLE
> Why not let him try? If he's wrong, there's still this.

He takes up the silver bullet.

> TALBOT
> But there's something so - so repulsive about that man!

On the line he EXITS toward the window o.s. Anatole looks after him and says dryly:

> ANATOLE
> Apparently life doesn't mean as much to you as you said - nor Yvonne.

163   INT. KITCHEN - MED. - DAY

at window. Talbot us approaching window at the end of
Anatole's line. He turns and looks back at the other
o.s., angry at the implication.

> ANATOLE'S VOICE
> (o.s.)
> If they did, you'd go to Dracula
> - if he were the devil himself!

Talbot seems to find it hard to meet the other's eyes. He
turns back and looks out thru the window. After a moment
he asks:

> TALBOT
> How do I reach that old
> moth-eaten castle of his?

164   INT. KITCHEN - MED. - DAY

on Anatole.

> ANATOLE
> Follow the path that leads around
> the first low hill.

165   INT. KITCHEN - MED. - DAY

on Talbot at window. For a moment he hesitates, then
moves to the door and opens it. He looks out for an
instant, then with a glance back at Anatole, he EXITS,
obviously on his way to Dracula.

166   INT. KITCHEN - MED. - DAY

on stair landing. The door opens a few inches and Yvonne
peeks out. Seeing that Talbot has gone, her eyes brighten
Presumable she has been in on what Anatole has been trying to do with Talbot - possibly has been listening back
of the closed landing door. She glances at her father,
then off after Talbot as she says:

> YVONNE
> Were you able to convince him,
> father?

As she finishes the line, CAMERA PANS to Anatole and
DOLLIES IN CLOSE on him.

> ANATOLE
> (gravely)
> Yes - I convinced him

As he ends the line, he takes up the silver bullet, sets
it at the muzzle of the old gun and rams it home with the
ramrod. The implication is fairly obvious; he has con-
vinced Talbot but is himself not so sure.

167 STOCK SHOT OF CASTLE
(LONG SHOT of MINIATURE from "Wolfman Meets Frankenstein."

DISSOLVE TO:

168 ext. castle - moat - full - day
gates of castle and drawbridge upstage. Talbot ENTERS
not sure of which way he should go. He climbs to drawbridge and looks into the courtyard within, hesitates,
then ENTERS doubtfully.

169 INT. COURTYARD - FULL - DAY
Talbot ENTERS through gates, surveys the dilapidated
scene dubiously. Talbot crosses thru the graves toward
the door leading into the castle, pausing en route to
look casually at a headstone or two.

170 EXT. CASTLE DOOR - MED. DAY

Talbot climbs the few steps to the landing before the door
Laying hold of the latch, he swings the heavy, creaking
door open and steps inside.

171 INT. CASTLE CORRIDOR - MED. - DAY

at door. Talbot ENTERS looking about on all sides at the
appearance of ruin and disuse. CAMERA PANS or DOLLIES
with him as he moves a few paces thru the fallen masonry.
Sections of the roof have apparently fallen in for there
are hot sunspots here and there on the walls. It is too
badly tumbled down to be the proper entrance. He looks
about uncertainly, the calls:

TALBOT
Count Dracula!

Back from all sides comes the echo of his words, a chorus
of ghostly voices that seem to mock him. Obviously this
is not a customary entrance to the castle. He turns and
is about to retrace his steps, when something at the far
end of the corridor catches his attention. He changes
his mind and starts toward it, CAMERA PANNING him through
the fallen timbers and rubble. At the extreme end of the
room is the door through which we previously saw the bat
fly.

172	INT. CASTLE CORRIDOR - MED. - DAY
at door. Talbot ENTERS. He listens to see if he can hear any sound of life beyond. His eyes fall on the heavy latch of the door. In contrast to everything else in the place, the metal is free of dust which he determines by rubbing a finger tentatively over its surface. He knocks lightly on the door. There is no response. Again he calls:

		TALBOT
	Count Dracula.

and again the echoes reverberate in the emptiness. He tries the door tentatively. It opens and he peers into the next room. What he sees rather surprises and relieves him. He ENTERS.

173	INT. LIVING QUARTERS - MED. - DAY
at door. Talbot ENTERS and looks about. CAMERA PANS him to a position that gives us a good view of the room. In contrast to the other parts of the castle through which we have passed, this room is in good repair. The walls are of masonry, but the ceiling is intact, supported by heavy pillars of stone. The floor is flagstone but is partially covered by rich rugs. The walls are of stone but the crudeness is also relieved by occasional rich tapestries and heavy and rather mournful oil paintings. The windows in the room are high and small, giving the place a dark and not too pleasant an atmosphere. A beautiful, heavy old square piano is the main piece of furniture in the room and it is open as if it has been played on recently. Besides this there are a couple of old period pieces of furniture. At the end of the room opposite the door through which Talbot entered is another door leading still deeper into the castle.

174	INT QUARTERS - MED. - DAY
on Talbot as he looks about curiously on all sides. The set up of ruined corridors and comfortable quarters grows more and more interesting if bewildering to him. He EXITS toward the second door.

175	INT. LIVING QUARTERS - MED. - DAY
at second door. Talbot ENTERS to it. Like the other door to these quarters, this one's latch is dustless. Talbot knocks rather diffidently, receives no response and again decides to go on in anyway. He opens the door and EXITS thru it.

176 INT. LIBRARY - MED. FULL - DAY
The architecture of this room differs but little from the one Talbot just left, but its furnishings are quite different. Its flagstoned floor is covered by rugs as in the other, but its walls are lined from floor to ceiling with shelves all filled with books - thousands of them, mostly old volumes with leather bindings. In some places cobwebs have gathered over them - the ones not ordinarily. There is a fireplace, heavy and of massive stone construction like the balance of the building, but it seems not to have been much used. A few charred logs are half buried in dust and ashes giving it a lifeless and uninviting appearance. The furnishings are meagre but rich. There is an enormous carved table which apparently serves all purposes. Obviously the Count uses it as a study table. There are handwritten papers scattered about and an accumulation of old, musty volumes, one or two of which are opened. There are inkwells and pens and a couple of retorts in racks over unlighted alcohol burners. A few dusty bottles of chemicals are also in evidence. Talbot ENTERS from living quarters, looks about room, again calls Dracula without answer. Now he moves out toward an o.s. door.

177 INT. LIBRARY - MED. DAY
at second door. Talbot ENTERS, opens door and looks out into the next room.

178 INT. SECOND CASTLE CORRIDOR - FULL - DAY
from Talbot's angle. It is in the same state of disuse and general dilapidation that characterized the first corridor. Dust, fallen rubble, cobwebs with streaks of sunlight falling thru the broken roof above.

       TALBOT'S VOICE
     (o.s.)
   Count Dracula!

Again the mocking echoes whose vibrations cause a few thin trickles of fine dust to drop from above through the sun spots.

179 INT. LIBRARY - MED. SHOT - DAY
on Talbot at second door. He closes it and turns to go.

180   INT. LIBRARY - MED. FULL - DAY
      Talbot ENTERS from o.s. door. He starts toward the one
      through which he originally entered but stops before he
      gets to it, and prompted by a natural curiosity, moves
      to a section of book shelves and starts running over the
      titles. Now he sees the open books on the desk-table
      and idly glances at them. He makes a double-take as he
      notices the titles. One of them is an exhaustive treatis
      on lycanthropy; the other is "Supernatural Manifestations
      and as a sub-head, "Demons, Vampires, Werewolves."

181   INT. LIBRARY - MED. CLOSE - DAY
      on Talbot as he realizes he has two authoritative books
      on his own case - the scientific and the superstitious.
      He thumbs through the pages as an idea grows on him.
      Now he sits at the table and, taking up a pen, starts to
      write a note.

182   INSERT - CLOSE
      on hand as it finishes signing note, the context of which
      is:

                    Count Dracula
                         I need your help.
                    Please see me today, however late.
                    Time is growing short

                                        Lawrence Talbot

                                                    FADE OUT

      FADE IN

183   INT. KITCHEN - CLOSE - NIGHT
      on wall clock, time - a few minutes after four a.m.
      CAMERA PULLS BACK from clock and PANS to Talbot who sits
      at the table wearily studying one of the two books he has
      borrowed from Dracula and which lie on the table before
      him. He is tired and discouraged. He lifts his head
      sharply as he HEARS a slow, measured KNOCK at the door.
      His eyes show eagerness as he says:

                         TALBOT
                    Come in!

184   INT KITCHEN - MED. - NIGHT
      at door as it opens and Dracula ENTERS with a slight bow.

                                                    CONTINUED

184 CONTINUED

                    DRACULA
          I found your note. I'm sorry
          I was not in when you called.

As he speaks he is moving out toward Talbot.

185 INT. KITCHEN - MED. - NIGHT
     on Talbot. As he rises, the Count is entering.

                    TALBOT
          It's so late I'd about given you
          up Count.

                    DRACULA
          It's my duty to help anyone I can-
          regardless of the hour. I take it
          you're sincere in asking my help/

                    TALBOT
                (miserably)
          Yes. Everything you predicted has
          come true. I don't want to die! I
          want to live! That's why I borrowed
          these - I thought they might help me.

He indicates the books. Dracula takes one up.

                    DRACULA
          Vampires - werewolves.

He laughs contemptuously and tosses it back to the table where it flops open.

                    DRACULA
          Rubbish! What you need is a
          doctor - as I told you before.

He moves upstage to fireplace, Talbot following speaking.

                    TALBOT
          That's why I was looking for you.
          You will help me won't you? Anatole
          says that you are also a doctor!

                    DRACULA
                (hopefully)
          Of course - of course. Why else would
          I come here at this unearthly hour.

                    TALBOT
                (hopefully)
          And you really believe you can?

                                        CONTINUED

185 CONTINUED

                    DRACULA
               (matter-of-factly)
          Beyond any doubt.
               (smiles thinly)
          Naturally there remains the
          question of payment.

                    TALBOT
               (losing hope)
          But I've got no money. You know
          that. You said I could . . .

                    DRACULA
               (smiling reassuringly)
          Don't be alarmed. All I require is
          a - shall we say "token payment?"

186 INT. KITCHEN - CLOSE - NIGHT
     on Dracula. His lips are smiling but his eyes bore into
     Talbot's o.s.

                    DRACULA
          Yvonne wears a little cross at
          her throat. I should like that cross . . .
          nothing more.

187 INT. KITCHEN - CLOSE - NIGHT
     on Talbot. He regards the Count with a puzzled
     frown.

                    TALBOT
          Yvonne's crucifix? That's a
          strange request.

188 INT. KITCHEN - MED - NIGHT
     on the two men. dracula

               (smiling sarcastically)
          Surely it's not too high a price for
          curing you. You can buy another like
          it for two kronen.

                    TALBOT
          I know - but I have an uneasy feeling
          that - - -

He leaves the sentence dangling and his eyes go to the
door leading to the upper rooms.
                    DRACULA
               (suavely)
          There is not too much time, you know.
          Tomorrow night brings the full moon and-
          - -

                                             CONTINUED

188 CONTINUED

Talbot's eyes come back to the Count with a jerk and in them we see the fear this thought brings with it. The Count presses his advantage.

> DRACULA
> You could get it now, while she's asleep - it would be quite simple.

> TALBOT
> (mumbling)
> Yes - I suppose I could.

> DRACULA
> Of course, if you do not require my services . . .

He starts to leave.

> TALBOT
> (stopping him)
> Wait! I'll get it!

He crosses quickly to the foot of the stairs, where he glances back uncertainly, then goes up and thru the door to the upper rooms. CAMERA PANS HIM

189 INT. KITCHEN - CLOSE - NIGHT
on Dracula looking after Talbot. With a smile of triumph he EXITS quickly to the door leading to the compound.

190 INT. YVONNE'S ROOM - MED. FULL - NIGHT
The room is lighted by a small lamp on a stand near the head of the bed where Yvonne lies asleep. The corridor opens and Talbot ENTERS. He crosses to the bed, regards the sleeping girl a moment, then bending over, starts to unfasten the chain that holds the cross at her throat.

191 INT YVONNE'S ROOM - MED. CLOSE - NIGHT
at window. The window is closed. The big bat flies into scene and flutters outside the glass watching Talbot inside.

192 INT. YVONNE'S ROOM - MED. FULL - NIGHT
Talbot straightens with the cross and quietly leaves the room.

es

193 INT. YVONNE'S ROOM - MED. CLOSE - (TRICK SHOT) - NIGHT
at window. The bat is on as before. It DISSOLVES into
a wisp of vapor which starts to seep in through the crack
under the window.

194 INT. KITCHEN - MED. FULL NIGHT
The door to stair landing opens and Talbot enters with
the cross. He stops short as he sees the Count has
gone. Closing the door he calls softly:

              TALBOT
Count Dracula.

Getting no answer, he comes down the stairs and crosses
to the outer door.

195 INT. KITCHEN - MED. NIGHT
at compound door. Talbot opens the door, and
stepping outside again calls o.s.

            TALBOT'S VOICE
              (o.s.)
Count Dracula.

196 INT. YVONNE'S ROOM - MED. FULL - (TRICK SHOT) NIGHT
Yvonne asleep as before. The last of the vapor is coming
in under the window and forming into a small cloud which
disforms into a bat which flies over the bed, hovers a
moment, then settles to the bed clothing and starts working its way up toward the girl's throat.

197 INT. YVONNE'S ROOM - MED. - NIGHT
Shadowgraph of girl in silhouette against the wall at far
side of bed, the shadow cast by the lamp on the bed stand.
In shadow we see the chittering bat work its way up to
her throat.

198 INT. KITCHEN - MED. - NIGHT
at compound door. Talbot enters puzzled, closes the door
and starts toward the fireplace unable to explain the
Count's absence. He pauses by the table where he was
reading earlier. He glances down at the open book as he
turns away, makes a double take as something on the page
attracts his attention. He turns back quickly to it and
spreading the pages stares down at the text/

199 INSERT - CLOSE
on a paragraph on page of book

> "The vampire doth appear in
> many forms, and there hath
> been found but one infallible
> safeguard against his attack
> namely the Sacred Cross."

200 INT. KITCHEN - MED. CLOSE - NIGHT
on Talbot as he finishes reading from the book spread on the table before him. His eyes rise from it as the full implication strikes home. The Cross! The thing he has just taken from Yvonne's throat! Such a strange request -- and now Count Dracula has disappeared! Is it possible that --? He springs up the stairs to the door and disappears thru it.

201 INT. YVONNE'S ROOM - MED. AT DOOR - NIGHT

It is thrown open and Talbot enters. He stops short and stares off at the bat at Yvonne's at Yvonne's throat. Now he rushes out toward it.

202 INT. YVONNE'S ROOM - MED. - NIGHT

on shadowgraph on wall of the bat at Yvonne's throat. It spreads its wings and flies up out of scene as Talbot rushes in and follows it with his eyes.

203 INT. YVONNE'S ROOM - MED. FULL - NIGHT

Talbot stands staring as the thin, wispy vapor is drawn out thru the crack under the window. Yvonne is stirring restlessly, as if half-awake. Talbot steps quickly to her side and sitting on the edge of the bed, takes her gently by the shoulders.

204 INT. YVONNE'S ROOM - MED. CLOSE - NIGHT
on Talbot and Yvonne as he shakes her gently and says:

TALBOT
Yvonne! Yvonne - what has happened?

The girl opens her eyes and looks vacantly at him, like a sleep-walker. They move from his face to other parts of the room as if searching for something or someone. Again he shakes her as if to rouse her can calls her name. She interrupts him in a strangely detached voice

CONTINUED

204   CONTINUED

                    YVONNE
            Yes, I can hear you now --
            Count Dracula.

From o.s. comes the SOUND of Anatole's VOICE.

                    ANATOLE'S VOICE
            Count Dracula! What is she talking
            about?

205   INT. YVONNE'S ROOM - MED. - NIGHT
      at door. Anatole has evidently just come in in time to
      hear what the girl said. He has his night shirt on, the
      tail tucked carelessly into the waistband of his pants.
      In one hand he holds a lighted candle, his tosseled hair
      suggesting he has been roused from his sleep.

                    ANATOLE
            What does it mean?

As he speaks he crosses to the bedside CAMERA PANNING him
till he stops bedside Talbot looking down at the girl.

                    TALBOT
            I'm afraid it means you good
            friend Count Dracula is one of the
            un-dead - a vampire!

                    ANATOLE
                (irritable)
            How can you talk such nonsense?

                    TALBOT
            When I came in here, there was a
            bat - a huge one - at Yvonne's
            throat.

                    ANATOLE
                (looking about skeptically)
            So? Where is it now?

                    TALBOT
            I don't know. It seemed to - to
            melt into thin air.

                    ANATOLE
            You don't expect me to believe
            such - such madness?
                    TALBOT
                (quietly)
            Are you sure it's madness? Look
            at those tiny wounds on her throat

                                        CONTINUED

es

205   CONTINUED

Anatole sets down the candle and moves closer to look at the place Talbot has indicated.

206   INSERT: CLOSE
on Yvonne's throat. Two discolored discs perhaps an inch apart show plainly on the skin over the jugular vein. They are not open wounds, but more like blotches with a tiny puncture at the center.

207   INT. YVONNE'S ROOM - MED. - NIGHT
on group as Anatole raises his eyes from the wounds. He is obviously impressed in spite of himself. Before he can speak, Talbot takes up the conversation.

                    TALBOT
          When the vampire takes the form of
          a bot, it leaves that sort of wound
          where it draws blood from its
          victim.

during this Yvonne has lain as before, eyes open, but staring sightlessly and apparently listening to something unheard by the others.

                    YVONNE
          Sh! Be quiet, please, so I can hear.

Talbot and Anatole turn to her anxiously. She ignores them as she listens with absorption. Then smiles and nods.

                    YVONNE
          Yes --yes --- of course I shall
          come to you -- yes, at sunset.

208   INT. YVONNE'S ROOM - NIGHT

on Anatole and Talbot. Their eyes meet.

                    TALBOT
          If she meets him tonight, she will
          become one of the un-dead, a loathe-
          some thing like himself, to live with
          out a soul through all eternity!

                    ANATOLE
          You don't believe that!

                                        CONTINUED

208   CONTINUED

                    TALBOT
          Believe it! If I hadn't listened
          to you and your scientific drivel,
          this would not have happened!

He looks at the girl, then continues:

                    TALBOT
          However, there is one sure way
          to protect her against him.

He lifts the cross so Anatole can see it, then turns to put it on Yvonne.

209   INT YVONNE'S ROOM - MED. - NIGHT

on group. Talbot takes one end of the chain in each hand and reaches out to put it on Yvonne's throat. For the first time she seems to become conscious of the two men. Her eyes widen at sight of the cross, then covering her eyes with her hands she cries hysterically:

                    YVONNE
          No, no! You mustn't! A Crucifix --
          it would destroy me!

Handing the chain to Anatole, Talbot pulls the girl's hands down as he tells Anatole:

                    TALBOT
          Here! She's got to wear it! It's
          the only thing Dracula fears!

Despite Yvonne's struggles, he gets her hands down so Anatole can fasten the chain in place.

210   INT. YVONNE'S ROOM - VERY CLOSE - NIGHT

on Yvonne as Anatole's hands fasten the chain at her throat. Suddenly her eyes lose their wild look, her head sags limply and she collapses.

211   INT. YVONNE'S ROOM - MED. - NIGHT

on the three. Yvonne has fallen limply and awkwardly to one side where she lies motionless, the two men staring at her.

                    ANATOLE
          What is it, Larry? What's happening

                                        CONTINUED

211 CONTINUED

As he speaks he starts working at the chain to get the cross off, talking as he works.

                TALBOT
        Dracula has done his work well! He's
        taken the first steps toward making
        her like himself.

By this time he gets the cross away from the girl's throat and passes it to Anatole without looking at him as he free hand reaches for her wrist to try her pulse.

212 IN YVONNE'S ROOM - CLOSE - NIGHT

on Anatole and Talbot. The latter sits with his hand on the girl's wrist counting the pulse. His tension relaxes somewhat and he says:

                TALBOT
        She'll be all right for a while - - -
        but she's still in danger.

213 INT. YVONNE'S ROOM MED. FULL - NIGHT

as Talbot speaks he is rising and starting to make the semi-conscious girl comfortable. As he draws the covers up about her he continues speaking to Anatole.

                TALBOT
        Get dressed and come downstairs.
        We've got a lot to do and not
        much time to do it.

                              DISSOLVE TO

214 INT. KITCHEN - CLOSE - DAY
on Talbot seated at the table, resting his elbows on it as he reads from one of the books borrowed from the Count.

                TALBOT
        (reading aloud)
        "By night the un-dead - the vampire -
        assumeth one of many forms. At times
        he appeareth as a bat; and again as a
        wolf
        roaming the countryside, seeking whom
        he may devour. And against him the
        strength of man availeth naught. But
        from dawn till sunset he must remain
        in his coffin. There he may be sought
        out and destroyed - by driving through
        his heart a stake of consecrated wood."

                              CONTINUED

es

214 CONTINUED
As Talbot is reading, the CAMERA DRAWS BACK to include Anatole who sits with his elbows on his knees and his chin cupped in his hands listening. Talbot finishes reading, lets the book close and looks at the older man for reaction. Anatole rises to his feet with a shake of the head.

      ANATOLE
    But's it's fantastic. According to
    science it's - -

Talbot hotly interrupts.

      TALBOT
    It's superstition! That's what
    science calls everything it can't
    explain!

He leaps to his feet and crossing to Anatole, faces him.

215 INT. KITCHEN - MED. - DAY

on Anatole and Talbot.

      TALBOT
    Can science deny your daughter is
    in her room, half crazed by the
    sight of the Holy Cross?

Anatole shakes his head. Talbot rushes on:

      TALBOT
    Can it explain the bat I saw at
    her throat? Or deny the wounds
    it left there?

      ANATOLE
    No - I suppose not.

      TALBOT
    I tell you Count Dracula is really
    the un-dead. Everything points to it.

216 INT. KITCHEN - CLOSE - DAY

on Talbot

      TALBOT
     (continues gravely)
    We've got to find his coffin before
    sunset, Anatole - and destroy him
    in it.

es

INT. KITCHEN - CLOSE - DAY

    on Anatole. He shakes his head with a wry smile.

                    ANATOLE
           In that tumbled-down castle?
           That's a large order.

218   INT KITCHEN - MED. - DAY

on the two.

                      TALBOT
           Go to Slavno and get help from
           the police.

                    ANATOLE
               (ironically)
           Do you expect them to believe me?

                      TALBOT
           No. But they can't refuse to help.
           People in the district have been
           killed by a wolf - and there are
           no wolves here.

219   INT. KITCHEN - CLOSE - DAY

on Talbot.

                      TALBOT
           That's more of Dracula's work -
           throwing suspicion on me, to turn
           it away from himself.

220   INT. KITCHEN - MED - DAY

                    ANATOLE
               (unconvinced)
           It can do no harm to try.

Talbot grips his arm.

                      TALBOT
           We must do more than try. Tonight
           is the full moon, remember...and
           you'll have a werewolf to contend with!
           - - - as well as Dracula!

As Anatole nods and starts for the door,

                                             DISSOLVE TO

at 93

221 EXT. POLICE HEADQUARTERS SLAVNO - MED. DAY

on a crude cart standing before the entrance to the police station. A peasant and his wife stand by tearfully watching as a couple of uniformed men remove the covered body of a girl from the cart and carry it in through the doorway. A group of townspeople have gathered and there is the usual buzz of comment among them. CAMERA PANS with the body and DOLLIES IN CLOSE on sign beside the door establishing the building as Police Station (in Bohemian).

DISSOLVE

222 INT. COMMISSIONER'S OFFICE - MED. CLOSE - DAY
on Commissioner. He is smiling tolerantly at Anatole o.c.

COMMISSIONER
Surely you can't expect me to believe anything so preposterous, Anatole! This is the twentieth century!

CAMERA PULLS BACK during the speech to show Anatole facing the man across a large table. A uniformed policeman stands nearby at attention and a civilian clerk or two.

ANATOLE
I'm not sure I even believe it myself, sir. But everything points to it - even the man's name evokes the legend of what happened in London a few years ago.

The Commissioner takes up a pencil and prints some letters on a sheet of paper.

223 INSERT - CLOSE
on paper as a hand finishes printing in capital letters:

D R A C U L A

Now the pencil scratches out the name.

224 int. commissioner's office - close - day
on Commissioner staring down at the name and impressed in spite of himself. However, he is a hardheaded police officer. He shakes off his surprise and madding the paper, looks up at Anatole with a smile.

CONTINUED

at   94

224 CONTINUED

                        COMMISSIONER
              I think we can safely charge that
              to coincidence.

He tosses the paper into a basket.

225 INTO. COMMISSIONER'S OFFICE - CLOSE - DAY
     on Anatole

                        ANATOLE
              But several of my neighbors have
              been killed by a wolf - yet there
              are no wolves. That's not
              coincidence.

226 INT. COMMISSIONER'S OFFICE - MED. - DAY

The Commissioner smiles indulgently.

                        COMMISSIONER
              If your neighbors have been killed
              by wolves, there ARE wolves.

                        ANATOLE
                   (rising with a sigh)
              I had hoped you'd send men to
              investigate, sir - even if you
              were skeptical.

                        COMMISSIONER
              It's our job to protect the
              people from criminals - not
              witches and hobgoblins.

                        ANATOLE
              But my daughter -

                        COMMISSIONER
                   (interrupting)
              She's suffering from some mild
              hysteria. What she needs is a
              doctor - not a police escort.
              Good day, Anatole.

Anatole mutters a "good day" and EXITS

227 INT. COMMISSIONER'S OFFICE - MED. - DAY
     at door. Anatole ENTERS. As he starts to open the door
     a middle-aged man in physician's smock ENTERS rather
     excitedly.

                                                     CONTINUED

227   CONTINUED

ANATOLE
How do you do, Dr. Franz?

FRANZ
Hello, Anatole.

He hurries on out toward the Commissioner. Anatole starts through the doorway but stops and looks back with interest as he hears:

FRANZ' VOICE (O.S.)
A peasant has just come in with one of his children - the victim of another wolf attack.

anatole waits to hear more.

228   INT. COMMISSIONER'S OFFICE - MED. - DAY
at commissioner's desk. The doctor is facing the officer.

COMMISSIONER
Dead?

DOCTOR FRANZ
(nodding)
Throat torn out - like all the others.

COMMISSIONER
It looks as if I'd better organize the countryside for a wolf hunt.

FRANZ
I'm not so sure it is a wolf!

COMMISSIONER
What do you mean?

229   INT. COMMISSIONER'S OFFICE - MED. - DAY
on Anatole standing beside door. He reacts as Franz speaks o.s.

FRANZ' VOICE (O.S.)
I'm about half-convinced it's a man!

230   INT. COMMISSIONER'S OFFICE - MED. - DAY
on Commissioner and Franz.

CONTINUED

230 CONTINUED

> FRANZ
> Remember that case in Vasaria -
> the homicidal maniac that killed
> the interne.

> COMMISSIONER
> Yes, but - -

> FRANZ
> The attacks around here started
> shortly after he escaped. And he
> has never been caught, you know.

231 INT. COMMISSIONER'S OFFICE _ MED. - DAY

on Anatole at door. OVER SCENE COMES FRANZ' VOICE

> FRANZ' VOICE
> The wounds inflicted seem to be
> identical.

As he is speaking Anatole EXITS toward the speaker.

232 INT. COMMISSIONER'S OFFICE - MED. - DAY
on Commissioner and Franz

> COMMISSIONER
> It's possible, of course, but - -

Anatole ENTERS and interrupts

> ANATOLE
> (interrupting)
> When was this murder committed
> in Vasaria, Doctor Franz?

> FRANZ
> About a month ago - - the nigh
> of the last full moon.

> ANATOLE
> Have you a description of him,
> Mr. Commissioner?

> COMMISSIONER
> (curtly)
> The fugitive is a man, Anatole -
> not a vampire, nor a werewolf.

CONTINUED

232   CONTINUED

                    ANATOLE
               (with quiet dignity)
          I asked a civil question. I've
          a right to an answer.

                    FRANZ
          Why do you want to know?

                    ANATOLE
          I'm afraid I may know where to
          find him.

Both Franz and the Commissioner react in surprise at
this and Franz says:

                    FRANZ
          The police sent us reward notices.

                    COMMISSIONER
          Yes. I should have one in my desk.

As he speaks he is fishing through papers in the desk.
He finds what he is after and passes it over to Anatole
who stares down at it.

233   INSERT - CLOSE
       on police reward notice in Bohemian. It is a description
       of Talbot and in the center is a picture of Talbot as
       photographed by the reporters the night he was found on
       the ground with the skeleton of the girl. Most of the
       girl has been eliminated before the cut was made.

234   INT. COMMISSIONER'S OFFICE - MED. - DAY

       Anatole looks up from the poster and nods.

                    ANATOLE
          I'm sorry to say I know where you
          can find him.

                    COMMISSIONER
          Where?

                    ANATOLE
          At my home. He married my daughter.

He turns to Franz and continues:

                    ANATOLE
          I've had reason to believe he is
          a lycanthrope.

                                        CONTINUED

at

234 CONTINUED

> COMMISSIONER
> (to policeman)
>
> Send three men with Anatole to
> bring in the criminal.

The policeman salutes and as they start out,

> DISSOLVE

235 INT. YVONNE'S ROOM - MED. CLOSE - DAY

on Yvonne. She is in bed, here eyes staring off with a faraway look. CAMERA DOLLIES BACK to include Talbot standing near the foot of the bed watching her. The SOUND of a clock STRIKING three somewhere in the house, causes him to lift his head, listening. He crosses to the window and looks out for some sign of Anatole returning. Not seeing him, he EXITS to the corridor.

236 INT. KITCHEN - MED. FULL - DAY

as Talbot ENTERS from upstairs. He hurries to the desk where he sits down and starts to write a short note. He rises and lays the note on the table where it will be readily seen, then hurries out into compound.

237 INSERT - CLOSE
on handwritten note:

> Anatole:
> I do not dare wait
> longer. Have gone to the
> castle.
>
> Talbot

> DISSOLVE TO

238 EXT. CASTLE - FULL - DUSK
Talbot ENTERS, looks about at ill-kept graves then goes on INTO castle.

239 INT. RUINED CORRIDOR - FULL - DUSK
Talbot ENTERS from outside - starts looking about in debris for sign of a doorway that may lead to what he hopes to find.

> WIPE TO

at   99

240   EXT. COMPOUND - DULL - DUSK

      Anatole and three men riding up the road at fast gait.
      CAMERA PANS THEM INTO the compound where they pull up.

241   EXT. COMPOUND - MED. - DUSK
      on group. Anatole dismounts.

                              ANATOLE
                            (to others)
                      Wait here. I'll bring him out.

      He EXITS to house.

424   INT. KITCHEN - MED. FULL - DUSK

      Anatole ENTERS, looks about, then calls:

                              ANATOLE
                      Larry!

      Getting no answer he hurries to the stairs and goes up to
      the landing, opens the door and calls upstairs:

                              ANATOLE
                      Larry!
      Goes on upstairs.

243   INT. YVONNE'S ROOM - MED. - DAY

      at hall door. In the hallway outside Anatole is heard
      calling:

                              ANATOLE'S VOICE
                            (through door)
                      Larry, are you up here?

      The door opens quietly and Anatole looks in curiously. He
      reacts at what he sees PAST CAMERA and starts forward a
      couple of steps INTO the room as if to assure himself he
      has seen aright. As he moves forward CAMERA PULLS QUICKLY
      BACK to include the bed. The covers are thrown back and
      Yvonne is gone. For a moment Anatole stands speechless,
      then he hurries back into the corridor and calls:

                              ANATOLE
                      Yvonne! Yvonne, where are you?

      Getting no response, he hurries back toward the stairs.

at

244 INT. KITCHEN - FULL - DUSK

Anatole enters and searches about desperately. He then
notices the envelope that Larry had left for him.

245 INT. KITCHEN - MED. - DUSK
on Anatole as he opens the envelope and reads the note.

245 INT. KITCHEN - MED. - DUSK
CLOSE on Anatole's FACE as he reads and his eyes widen.

246 INT. KITCHEN - FULL - DUSK
As Anatole crumples the note in his hand. He EXITS into the
compound and speaks to the gendarmes.

247 EXT. COMPOUND - FULL - DUSK.
on gendarmes as Anatole ENTERS and speaks:

> ANATOLE
> (excitedly)
> Talbot is not here. He has gone to
> Dracula's Castle.

248 EXT. COMPOUND - MED. - DUSK
On group as gendarmes and Anatole mount their horses.

> ANATOLE
> We must hurry. He must have
> taken Yvonne with him. The sun
> is almost down and it will be
> too late!

249 EXT. COMPOUND - FULL - DUSK
As Anatole and the gendarmes gallop out of the compound
and ride in the direction of Dracula's Castle.

at

250   STOCK SHOT OF SUN NEARING HORIZON

        (Put bars across it in optical printer.)

                                                              CUT TO

251   INT. SECOND CASTLE CORRIDOR - MED. CLOSE - DUSK

        on Talbot looking off at window and sunset. OVER SCENE
        COME wild track of the girl's VOICE, speaking softly
        and in dead tones, repeating the words she spoke in her
        bedroom.

                            YVONNE'S VOICE (O.S.)
                        Yes, of course I'll come to you
                        at sunset.

        Talbot gets an idea - a new ray of hope. Turning he runs
        toward EXIT door, CAMERA PANNING HIM.

252   INT. DRACULA'S STUDY

        Talbot hurries in through door and CAMERA PANS HIM as he
        runs across it hurrying to get outside the castle.

253   EXT. HILL TRAIL - FULL - SUNSET
        Shot of Anatole and horsemen through at a run.

254   EXT. ENTRANCE TO CASTLE GROUNDS - MED. FULL SUNSET

        Yvonne ENTERS and makes her way rather like a sleepwalker
        to the grounds. WIND is beginning to move the trees near her

255   EXT. CASTLE GRAVEYARD - MED. FULL - SUNSET

        Yvonne ENTERS, eyes fixed ahead and moving like a sleep-
        walker. CAMERA PANS her on her way to castle door until
        it brings into foreground the figure of Talbot hidden be-
        hind a pile of fallen masonry or other shelter. He watches
        the girl as she continues her walk toward o.s. door. With
        a smile of triumph he turns and starts searching about
        among the debris near at hand. He finds and drags out
        from under the mass a slender cross - once a headstone -
        perhaps three foot in length. The fallen rubble has
        broken off the lower end, not straight across but in a
        long splintered break leaving the point very sharp. Taking
        this up he glances at it, shows his satisfaction and hurries
        out after the girl. From his movements it is hard to tell
        whether he is a menace to her safety or not.

at   102

256   INT. FIRST CASTLE CORRIDOR - MED. - SUNSET
      at entrance door. Yvonne is COMING IN through the door. It
      shelters her from the WIND which is now picking up outside.
      She walks unemotionally out PAST CAMERA...Talbot appears
      in the doorway, looks after her and follows after her,
      CAMERA PANNING HIM to show Yvonne disappearing through
      the upstage door to the living quarters. Talbot trails
      after her unobserved.

257   INT. LIVING QUARTERS - MED. FULL - SUNSET

      Yvonne ENTERS and crossing room EXITS to library. Talbot
      follows after her.

258   EXT. HILL TRAIL - FULL - SUNSET
      WIND is beating at Anatole and gendarmes riding hard through scene.

259   INT. SECOND CASTLE CORRIDOR - MED. FULL - SUNSET

      Yvonne ENTERS, unconscious she is being followed. She
      walks to center of room and Talbot appears at the doorway
      behind her watching . Now, for the first time, the girl
      appears to be a bit uncertain. She stops in the middle
      of the debris and looks about vacantly as if trying to
      decide which way to go.

260   INT. SECOND CASTLE CORRIDOR - MED. - CLOSE - SUNSET

      on Yvonne as she looks about. She turns her eyes back
      toward the door.

261   INT. SECOND CASTLE CORRIDOR - MED. - SUNSET

      on Talbot. He sees the girl's eyes turning his way and
      ducks out of sight behind some convenient cover in time
      to avoid being seen.

262   INT. SECOND CASTLE CORRIDOR - MED - FULL - SUNSET

      Yvonne realizes the way to go and moves to a pile of
      fallen masonry. She disappears through what looks like a
      shallow opening. Talbot hurries after her, peers thru the
      opening then EXITS through it.

263   INT. CIRCULAR TOWER - FULL - SUNSET
      Yvonne ENTERS at top of stairs and makes her way down.
      Talbot appears at head of stairs, watches till she has
      disappeared at foot of stairs and then quickly follows.

264 INT. CRYPT - FULL - SUNSET

On the platform are the two coffins, one open, the other closed. Sunlight from the o.s. source falls slanting upon them. Yvonne is halfway to the dais. Talbot ENTERS from CAMERA and stops in f.g., watching as she steps up beside the closed coffin and starts to lift the lid.

265 STOCK SHOT OF SUNSET

The sun has reached the horizon and is partially hidden below it.

266 INT. CRYPT - MED. - SUNSET
on Yvonne and coffin. She finishes raising the coffin's lid exposing Dracula lying inside with his eyes closed. The sun is still fairly strong on the two.

      YVONNE
  It is sunset, Count Dracula - and
  I am here - as I promised.

As the line ends, the sunlight fades from scene leaving the light flat.

267 INT. CRYPT - CLOSE - SUNSET

on Dracula in coffin. His eyes open slowly and as they focus on Yvonne o.s., a thin smile comes to his lips. Then they jerk to another spot and a look of terror comes to them. Instinctively his hands rise and he stands in the coffin.

268 INT. CRYPT - MED. - DAY

on Yvonne, CAMERA cutting above the coffin. Her eyes are staring rather sightlessly at nothing. Talbot steps in holding the cross high. He plunges down but Dracula moves too quickly. They HEAR an INHUMAN BLOOD CONGEALING CRY OF FURY, that seems to shake the very walls and to write such a look of horror on their faces. THE CAMERA too, effected by this sudden change, TURNS COMPLETELY AROUND FROM THEM TO HOLD IN A REVERSE ANGLE IN A MED. SHOT while the human form of Dracula changes into a HUGE BAT, churning the air with the angry swirl of its wings, his human cry of fury gives way to the angry CHITTERINGS of a monstrous thing... The, as if venting it's spleen upon the innocent CAMERA, the BAT power dives right for the LENS, VEILING EVERYTHING WITH IS HIDEOUS DIAPHANOUS WINGS.

at   104

269   CLOSE TWO SHOT - YVONNE AND TALBOT - FROM REVERSE
      ANGLE

      as they watch the Bat, amazed and petrified by the trans-
      formation that has taken place before their very eyes,
      as we HEAR o.s. Bat coming closer toward them. Talbot
      reaches to Yvonne, protectingly, takes her hand to force her behind
      him and using his body as a shield, he holds up the crucifix before
      him.

                        TALBOT
                  (whispering over his shoulder)
            Keep backing out....

      He has hardly finished this, when INTO THE PICTURE with
      a terrifying SCREECH dives the Bat right for him, as
      though to scratch his eyes out. Talbot HOLDING THE CRUCIFIX
      but the Bat is OUT OF THE PICTURE. THE CAMERA HOLDS ON THEM as they
      keep backing away toward the Living Room door, behind the CAMERA.

270   INT. LIVING ROOM - SHOOTING TOWARD OPEN DOOR OF LIBRARY -
      MED. CLOSE SHOT

      CAMERA PICKS UP FIRST, YVONNE and the TALBOT, their
      FACES TO CAMERA, as he tries to cover their retreat out
      of the room. In the b.g. fluttering in mid-air, as if
      getting set for another dive, is the Bat. Turning in
      the doorway to FACE CAMERA, Yvonne sees something o.s.
      which captures her attention -

                        YVONNE
                  (to Talbot; indicating
                   French doors in Living
                   Room)
            Through the garden there... it's
            quicker.

                        TALBOT
            Run for it...

271   LIVING ROOM - SHOOTING TOWARD FRENCH DOORS - MED. SHOT

      The gale outside has grown to great proportions, blowing
      the drapes of the French doors up into billowing waves, as
      Yvonne RUNS INTO SCENE as fast as she can and plunges
      into the garden and the HOWLING wind...on her EXIT, Talbot
      comes INTO SCENE...Seeing the Bat still coming for him, he
      makes a run for the French Doors just as the wind slams
      them closed...without stopping, Talbot crashes through the
      glass into the garden. He has hardly made it when right
      upon him the Bat appears flying INTO SCENE, in vengeful
      pursuit...

272 EXT. GARDEN - SHOOTING TOWARD THE FRENCH DOORS OF
     LIVING ROOM

The Wind is HOWLING through the trees and shrubbery. CAMERA MOVES INTO A CLOSE SHOT OF TALBOT, who is just getting to his feet, a little stunned by the shock shattered glass all around him. Yvonne, solicitously comes to his side. She is now fully rid of Dracula's control.

> YVONNE
> Are you hurt, darling?...
>
> TALBOT
> (rising to his feet)
> No...but we've got to hurry...

Talbot puts his arm about Yvonne and like Paul and Birginia, the classic lovers, they are on their way toward the garden Path, CAMERA TRUCKS BACK TO WIDER ANGLE OF GARDEN. For a moment the wind has abated, all seems quiet and peaceful, as the Moon sheds its light across the path...

273 EXT. GARDEN - MOVING TWO SHOT OF YVONNE AND TALBOT ALONG
     PATH

Yvonne sighs with relief, and looks up to heaven prayerfully...

> YVONNE
> (mumbling almost to
> herself, devoutly)
> Merci, Le Bon Dieu
>
> TALBOT
> We're not out of danger yet,
> dearest...
>   (looks up at the moon)
> You must get back home immediately...
>   (significantly)
> Before very long the climbing moon
> will win...

Suddenly the SCENE darkens.

274 FULL MOON - (STOCK SHOT) -

The rising Full moon is being blotted out by dark and ominous clouds.

275 EXT. GARDEN - MOVING CLOSE SHOT ON TALBOT AND YVONNE

The Wind which has abated, starts HOWLING again through the trees that border the path. And curiously the whole garden becomes suddenly dead, as though even the spirits of the graveyard have fled upon the ENTRANCE of the pursuing EVIL GIANT BAT.

In fact, Talbot turns just as THE BAT starts down on another one of his power dives. Talbot lifts the crucifix desperately trying to fight it off the Bat knocks the crucifix from his grip.

276 CLOSE GROUP SHOT - CRUCIFIX ON THE GROUND

Just as the Bat, attracted by the sight of blood from a deep scratch on the side of Talbot's face, closes in on him, Talbot now has only his hands to help him in his fight against the blood-thirsty Vampire... Yvonne starts for the crucifix. The Bat seeing this, turns to attack Yvonne... Talbot, realizing he is helpless to fight the Bat with his bare hands, makes a grab for the crucifix. Just as he is about to hold it up, the Bat flies OUT OF SCENE...CAMERA HOLDS ON TALBOT AND YVONNE.

     TALBOT
    (all concerned
     for Yvonne)
  Did he hurt you Yvonne?

     YVONNE
   (when noticing Talbot's
    face, frightenedly)
  Larry, your face is all
  scratched and bleeding.....

Yvonne quickly takes her handkerchief and tenderly starts to mop hi face...Gently he takes her arm down.

277 EXT. HILL PATH - FULL - NIGHT
On Anatole and the gendarmes riding at full speed to the CASTLE MINIATURE

             CONTINUED

277 CONTINUED

> TALBOT
> It's nothing....We can't delay
> here...He'll be back after us...

They start to hurry on, CAMERA HOLDS ON THEM, until they are lost from view around a clump of trees and bushes, when the Bat flies INTO THE SCENE, but instead of following after them, flies OUT OF SCENE AT AN ANGLE, as if, either to return to the Castle, or head them off.

278 MED. LONG SHOT - OF A PATH - SHOOTING TOWARD THE FOUNTAIN IN B.G.

Talbot and Yvonne hurry INTO SCENE from BEHIND CAMERA

> YVONNE
> (with a sigh of
> relief)
> We've lost him...Larry...

CAMERA TILTS UP ABOVE THEM, to show the BAT hanging from the branch of a tree, like some hideous loathsome thing, waiting to drop down upon them.

279 MED. CLOSE SHOT - SHOOTING DOWN FROM THE BAT'S ANGLE UPON THE PATH

We see the two approach CAMERA, hurrying on the path beneath. When suddenly Yvonne, tripping over some broken branch in the pathway, goes down on her knees. Instantly the Bat dives INTO THE PICTURE as if to pounce down upon her, when suddenly the Wind, which, by this time has been whipped up into cyclonic fury, starts sweeping the tree and its branches right across the SCENE, blotting all else from view...

280 EXT. MINIATURE GARDEN - NIGHT - SHOWING A TREE FALLING ACROSS THE SCREEN, uprooted by the Wind.

281 MED. WIDE ANGLE - TAKING IN THE PATH AND THE TREE

as if the hand of Providence has miraculously saved Yvonne and Talbot from Dracula, by dropping this uprooted tree between the pursued and the pursuer....

CONTINUED

282 MED. CLOSE SHOT OF BAT FLUTTERING TO ATTACK - NIGHT
As bat pulls himself up to it's full length and swoops
directly at Talbot and Yvonne

283 MED. FULL OF TALBOT AND YVONNE

as they see Dracula about to land on them.

284 MED. FULL SHOT OF BAT SWOOPING DIRECTLY INTO CAMERA
Talbot reacts by picking up crucifix. As Yvonne screams:

285 FULL SHOT - TRAIL - NIGHT

Talbot turns the crucifix around to the jagged edge and
pushes it swiftly into Dracula's heart.

286 MED. SHOT - ON THREE

As Dracula grabs at the crucifix but it is too late. His
wings crumple and he falls to the ground.

287 CLOSE ON DRACULA
as he lies dead. (TRICK SHOT) as he first turns back to his human for
then into a skeleton the bones of his fingers clutching the shaft of
the cross which is driven through his heart and then a pile of dust
which is blown away by the winds.

287A CLOSE ON GROUND showing crucifix lying in the dust and leaves

288 EXT. WOODED TRAIL OUTSIDE GARDEN - MED - NIGHT
on Talbot and Yvonne. She is staring down at the ghastly
sight on the ground. She turns and buries her face against
Talbot's shoulder, still in about half a faint.

289 ext. wooded trail outside garden - close
on Talbot and Yvonne.

> TALBOT
> We can't take any chances. We must
> go back and destroy his coffin.

He looks about, gets an idea, takes the girl in his arms
and hurries out with her.

290 INT. CRYPT MED. - FULL - NIGHT
SHOOTING AWAY from coffin. Talbot ENTERS carrying the
limp form of Yvonne. He deposits her on a slab of rock near
upstage wall, turns aside to drag out a long solid timber.

at

291   INT. CRYPT. FULL - NIGHT
        at raised platform. Talbot hurries in dragging the
        timber. He finds a vantage point and starts prying
        at one of the crumbling supports of the roof, intending
        to crash it down and bury Dracula's coffin.

292   EXT. GRAVEYARD - MED. FULL NIGHT

        Anatole and the gendarmes ENTER afoot. The latter have
        unslung their saddle carbines from the shoulders and
        are carrying them at the trail as they move uncertainly
        about among the graves.

293   INT. CRYPT - MED. FULL - NIGHT

        Talbot is still working at the pillar with his lever.
        Dust and small pebbles are trickling down as the pillar
        is shifted about by the action. Suddenly he gives a
        powerful heave and the pillar buckles. He drops the
        timber and runs back as the whole mass of disintegrat-
        ing masonry and rubble crashes down upon the coffins,
        burying them beyond hope of discovery.

294   EXT. IN GRAVEYARD - MED. FULL - NIGHT

        The gendarmes and Anatole are in a lose group in f.g.,
        standing listening as the last faint sounds of the cave-
        in die on the air.

                            SERGEANT
                    Sounded like an explosion!

                            FIRST GENDARME
                    Or a cave-in!

                            ANATOLE
                    Yvonne! She's in the castle!

                            SERGEANT
                            (pointing off)
                    The sound came from this way!

        He starts off at a trot, the other two following. Anatole
        protests.

                            ANATOLE
                    But my daughter!

        They pay no attention and hurry off around the building.
        Anatole hesitates, then hurries up the stairs and into
        the castle

at

295 INT. FIRST CORRIDOR - MED. FULL - NIGHT

Anatole ENTERS from outside, takes a couple of steps into the corridor, looks around and calls:

ANATOLE
Yvonne!

Only the echoes answer him. He moves on thru the debris toward o.s. door in living quarters.

296 INT. CRYPT - MED. FULL - NIGHT

on cave-in. Fine dust hangs in the air from the crash. Talbot stands in f.g. Now he turns and looks out PAST CAMERA, then hurries out toward where he left the girl.

297 INT. CRYPT - MED. FULL - NIGHT

Talbot runs in from camera and to the girl upstage on fallen masonry where he left her.

298 INT. CRYPT - MED. NIGHT
on Yvonne and Talbot. He sits on rock slab beside the girl and starts chafing her wrists trying to bring her back to consciousness.

299 INT. LIVING QUARTERS - MED. - NIGHT

Anatole ENTERS from first corridor. He stops and surveys the room in amazement. CAMERA PANS HIM to center of room to establish set. He looks about curiously, steps to a wall and lifts a tapestry to see if it may conceal a passageway. Finding non, he moves on toward the door to the next room.

300 INT. CRYPT - MED. - NIGHT
Talbot still trying to revive the girl without success. He looks off and up at stairs. Decides to get her out of the huge cavern-like room to the fresh air. He stoops and starts to lift her, then stops short staring down at the palm of her out-flung hand.

301 INSERT - CLOSE

on palm of Yvonne's hand, lying motionless, hanging over the edge of masonry. A pentagram dissolves into the palm.

302 INT. CRYPT - VERY CLOSE SHOT - NIGHT

on Talbot, staring down horrified at the pentagram as the full significance comes to him. Yvonne is to be his next victim. With a sob that sounds like a muffled: "Oh, God!" he covers his face with his hands and drops to his knees beside the girl, CAMERA TILTING DOWN WITH HIM to show him in f.g., with the girl's pale face beyond, as she lies unconscious on the rubble.

303 INT. LIBRARY - MED. FULL SHOT - NIGHT

Anatole leaves library and moves through doorway to the second corridor o.s.

304 INT. CRYPT - MED. SHOT - NIGHT

on Talbot kneeling beside th unconscious Yvonne, his eyes fixed almost hungrily on the girl's face, her one hand clasped between his own. This is goodbye and he knows it. For a moment he remains thus, then gently lowers the hand and rises to his feet, his eyes still on her face. CAMERA DOLLIES WITH HIM as he backs slowly away from her, then knowing the need for haste, he turns and runs out toward the stairs.

305 INT. SECOND CASTLE CORRIDOR - MED. FULL SHOT - NIGHT

Anatole disc. moving about the debris. He turns as if to retrace his steps back to the library. Then he stops and lifts his head listening. He turns back in the direction where we know the fallen masonry makes the unsuspected opening to the head of the circular stairs.

306 INT CIRCULAR STAIR TOWER - FULL SHOT - NIGHT

Talbot hurries in from o.s. crypt and runs up the stairway to the landing where he stops and turns to look back at Yvonne.

307 INT. STAIR TOWER - MED. SHOT - DAY

on upper landing. Talbot stands there looking off and down at the girl o.s. He backs slowly through the opening.

308 INT. SECOND CASTLE CORRIDOR - MED. SHOT - NIGHT

at opening to stairway. Talbot backs in through the opening. He hesitates just a second, then turns to hurry out but stops short in surprise

CONTINUED

308   CONTINUED

CAMERA DOLLIES QUICKLY BACK to include Anatole who stands facing him, the rifle held loosely in one hand. For a second neither speaks. Then:

> ANATOLE
> (accusingly)
> Where is Yvonne?

> TALBOT
> (pointing)
> Down there.

Anatole starts to pass him to go down to the girl. Talbot stops him.

> TALBOT
> Wait. Is that the gun with the silver bullet?

he indicates the rifle. Anatole nods.

> TALBOT
> Then use it - as I begged you to do the night I came to you.

> ANATOLE
> Why?

> TALBOT
> Tonight is the full moon - and Yvonne is marked for my victim. I saw the pentagram ion her palm!

> ANATOLE
> (deprecatingly)
> Surely you don't believe all that nonsense about pentagrams and werewolves and --

Talbot interrupts fiercely, grabbing Anatole by the arms and shaking him.

> TALBOT
> (interrupting)
> Why can't I make you believe what I know!

> ANATOLE
> Because I've found out all about you! I know you killed that interne in Vasaria. The gendarmes are waiting outside for you!

CONTINUED

cl

308 CONTINUED - 2

Talbot reacts to this news.

> TALBOT
> The gendarmes! I can't let them
> stop me! I've got to be miles from
> Yvonne by moon rise.
> ANATOLE
> Don't worry! They'll protect her
> from you!
> TALBOT
> But they can't hold me after I've
> become a......

he stops short as he realizes how they may detain him - keep him from doing the thing that is uppermost in his mind. vis., gets beyond reach of Yvonne so he can do her no injury. Now he clutches Anatole by the slack of his shirt front as he continues:

> TALBOT
> No matter what happens you stay
> with Yvonne, do you hear? Don't
> let her out of your sight! And
> when the time comes, use that
> silver bullet on me as you'd use
> it on a mad dog!

He turns to go. Anatole grabs him.

> ANATOLE
> But I can't let you --

He never finishes the sentence, because Talbot in an excess of desperation, grabs him and hurls him aside and rushes out toward the entrance to the castle.

309 INT. SECOND CASTLE CORRIDOR - MED. CLOSE SHOT - NIGHT

as Anatole falls INTO SCENE. He recovers and lifts his rifle to his shoulder to fire after the retreating Talbot.

310 INT. SECOND CASTLE CORRIDOR - MED. FULL SHOT - NIGHT

shooting toward door to the library, from Anatole's angle. Talbot is disappearing through the door into the other room and is too fast for Anatole to fire.

311 INT. SECOND CASTLE CORRIDOR - MED. SHOT - DAY
on Anatole as he lowers the rifle, then gets to his feet and hurriedly disappears through the opening to the top of the stairs to the crypt.

312   INT. CIRCULAR STAIR TOWER - FULL SHOT - NIGHT

Anatole ENTERS onto upper landing, SEES Yvonne below and o.s. He hurriedly descends the stairs to join her.

313   INT. CRYPT - MED. FULL SHOT - NIGHT

from angle of stairs. Yvonne lies as before on the crumbled masonry. Anatole RUNS IN FROM CAMERA and across to her.

314   INT. FIRST CASTLE CORRIDOR - MED. FULL SHOT - NIGHT

Talbot hurries IN from door to living quarters. He runs across to the door to the outside, throws it open and starts through, then stops short at what he SEES outside.

315   EXT. GRAVEYARD -
The three gendarmes are seen making their way toward the door through which Talbot is looking. They have not seen him.

316   INT. SECOND CASTLE CORRIDOR - MED. SHOT - NIGHT
at door. Talbot disc., looking outside. Seeing the gendarmes on their way in. He wants to hide, let them pass him and then escape to the outside and be on his way. He looks around wildly, then darts back of cover of fallen masonry as the three gendarmes ENTER looking about the ruin curiously. The sergeant turns to one of the men and says:

> SERGEANT
> Wait here. If he's inside he may
> try to get out this way.

The gendarme addressed salutes. The other two men make their way through the door into the living quarters. The guard starts rummaging about the debris casually, but does not get too close to where Talbot is hiding.

317   INT. LIVING QUARTERS - MED. FULL SHOT - NIGHT

Sergeant and gendarme ENTER and start looking about for Talbot, then EXIT into library.

318   INT. CRYPT - MED. SHOT - DAY

on Anatole and Yvonne. She comes to slowly, then her eyes widen in a horrified stare as she realizes part of what has happened

CONTINUED

318 CONTINUED

She draws back from Anatole, then recognising who it is, she clings to him. Anatole soothes her and asks quietly.

> ANATOLE
> What is it, Yvonne? What happened?

This brings the girl to a fuller recollection of events and she straightens to ask with a quick concern:

> YVONNE
> Where is Larry?

> ANATOLE
> (avoiding issue)
> He has gone. I'll tell you about it later. But where is Count Dracula?

This also brings back portions of what she has gone through.

> YVONNE
> Dracula! He was a VAMPIRE

She shudders at the recollection, then continues:

> YVONNE
> It was horrible! He's dead - Larry buried his coffin under that pile of rock and mortar!

She indicates the cave-in o.s. Anatole looks in the direction she points. He reacts.

> ANATOLE
> Coffin! Buried?

Not understanding the full implications of the girl's statement, Anatole leaves her and hurries out to investigate.

319 INT. CRYPT - MED. FULL SHOT - NIGHT

on cave-in as Anatole hurries to it and starts moving about it trying to find some sign of the coffin.

320 INT. FIRST CASTLE CORRIDOR - MED. FULL SHOT - NIGHT

Talbot still under cover. The guard, unconscious of his presence moves from the outer door toward the door to the living quarters, leaving the way clear for Talbot to get past him and effect his escape.

321 INT. FIRST CASTLE CORRIDOR - MED. SHOT

on Talbot. He is hidden behind some fallen masonry. His eyes follow the direction taken by the guard o.s. He realizes now is his chance and crouching starts to make his way toward the outer door, intent upon getting away. CAMERA PANS HIM as he moves toward the door. The movement brings him out of the gloom and into a sudden and unexpected square of light thrown in from o.s. He stops short and stares off toward the source of the light.

322 STOCK SHOT OF FULL MOON

It is just above the horizon

323 INT FIRST CASTLE CORRIDOR - CLOSE SHOT

on Talbot as the full horror of what is about to happen strikes him. The full moon. He is facing another trans
formation into a werewolf and nothing he can do will prevent it. His horror tells itself through his eyes as he stares off at the moon. Then in an excess of anguish, he covers his face with his forearms, rocking half hysterically. He ends by half falling, half-throwing himself to the ground, CAMERA TILTING WITH HIM to see him on the ground writhing.

324 INT. FIRST CASTLE CORRIDOR - MED. SHOT

on the guard. He HEARS the slight noise Talbot has made and turns to look about the room to see what caused it. he sees nothing, Talbot being hidden from him by rocks and debris.

325 INT. FIRST CASTLE CORRIDOR - MED. CLOSE SHOT

on Talbot, his face buried in his arms as he lies on the fallen mortar. He twists about and lowers his hands from his face as he stares off at the moon o.s. Now he grows calmer, continuing to stare off seemingly half hypnotised and resigned to what will happen.

326 INT. FIRST CASTLE CORRIDOR - VERY CLOSE (TRICK SHOT)

on Talbot as the metamorphosis takes place and he changes gradually from man to werewolf. At the end his lips curl and he jerks his eyes off in the direction of the guard o.s. He no longer wants to get out of the castle. He is intent on getting back to Yvonne. He crouches and moves off toward the guard.

cl

327   int. first castle corridor - med. full

The guard is over in the vicinity of the door to the living quarters. Talbot rises from the ground, and crouching low starts slipping toward the guard whose back is turned. Talbot takes a course that keeps him partially hidden from the guard by going from one bit of cover to another as he advances, the CAMERA PANNING HIM and finally bringing the guard into scene. The guard opens the door to the living quarters and looks inside. Talbot moves closer, slithering up to the top of a fallen rock slab.

338   INT. FIRST CASTLE CORRIDOR - CLOSE

on Talbot as he slides up to rock slab and prepares to attack the o.s. guard

339   INT. FIRST CASTLE CORRIDOR - MED.

shooting past Talbot in f.g., and showing the guard somewhat below as he closes the door to living quarters and turns to retrace his steps. He stops short, petrified with horror at sight of the werewolf poised above him ready to leap. For a second they remain thus, then the guard recovers his wits enough to start to raise the rifle. At this moment, Talbot leaps on him with a snarl and roar.

340   INT. SECOND CASTLE CORRIDOR - MED. FULL

The sergeant and gendarme disc. They have evidently been looking around for another exit and have found none.

                SERGEANT
There's no way out of here but
the way we came in.

He leads the way back toward the library door.

341   INT. FIRST CORRIDOR - MED.

on Talbot and sergeant. The struggle is about over and ends as Talbot hurls the man from him to fall limply on the masonry. Then Talbot turns to the living room door, opens it and scuttles through it.

342   INT. LIVING QUARTERS - MED

at door to corridor. Talbot springs in. He stops short at sight of something ahead.

F:

343 INT. LIVING QUARTERS - MED.

   at door to library. The sergeant and gendarmes are entering. As they close the door and start out past camera they stop short at sight of the werewolf o.s.

344 INT. LIVING QUARTERS - MED.

   on Talbot. He snarls and springs out past camera to attack.

345 INT. LIVING QUARTERS - FULL

   The sergeant and gendarme are at bay in front of the library door upstage. Talbot springs in from camera and charges toward them. Both raise their rifles and fire point blank at him. He doesn't even hesitate and is upon them before they can throw new cartridges into their guns.

346 INT. LIVING QUARTERS - MED.

   on sergeant and gendarme as Talbot leaps in, knocks the gendarme aside, and grappling with the sergeant starts to sink his teeth into his throat.

347 INT. LIVING QUARTERS - CLOSE

   on gendarme as he is knocked backwards into scene. He brings up against a wall, sees what is happening o.s., and clubbing his rifle brings it down in a full swing at the head of the werewolf.

348 INT. LIVING QUARTERS - CLOSE

   on Talbot and sergeant. Talbot has the latter on his knees and is bent over him snarling when the rifle butt swings into scene and crashes on his head. It does not even faze him. He drops the sergeant and turns to spring out at the gendarme.

349 INT. LIVING QUARTERS - MED.

   as Talbot lets the sergeant fall, and spinning on the gendarme knocks him sprawling. Then to avoid further delay, he whirls and disappears through the door to library. The sergeant and gendarme get groggily to their feet and give chase.

F:

350 INT. LIBRARY - MED.
At door to second corridor. Talbot runs in, throws the door open and looks back past camera. CAMERA SWINGS BACK and shows the sergeant and gendarme coming in from the living quarters. They are too late to throw other shots at the werewolf, but run out after him.

351 INT. SECOND CASTLE CORRIDOR - MED.

An opening to stair tower. Talbot runs in from camera, glances back, then starts in through the opening. CAMERA SWINGS BACK to library door and shows the sergeant and gendarme entering. It is obvious they have seen the werewolf go through the opening. They run after him.

352 INT. STAIR TOWER - MED.

on upper landing. Talbot comes in through the opening. He stops short and stares down toward Yvonne in the crypt o.s.

353 INT CRYPT. - FULL

from Talbot's angle. She sits alone looking off toward the cave-in, unaware of the presence of the werewolf.

354 INT. STAIR TOWER - MED.

on Talbot. He is looking down at Yvonne. With a muffled snarl he moves along the wall toward the stairs leading down. But he has no more than started, when a noise in the passageway behind him causes him to turn his eyes toward it. Now abandoning the attack on Yvonne for the moment, he turns back to the passage. As he gets a step into the opening he is met by the gendarme and the sergeant. With a roar he attacks them, but the quarters are confined and it is hard to work on them with the dispatch usual to him.

355 INT. CRYPT - MED.

on Yvonne. She is looking off at her father. Over the scene COMES THE SOUND of the SNARLS and the RACKET of the struggle at the head of the stairs. She looks up quickly in that direction.

F:

356 INT. STAIR TOWER - FULL

from Yvonne's angle. In the opening of the passageway may be seen Talbot's back as he struggles with the gendarmes, but from this distance and at the angle, his transformation is not apparent. Business is shot so his head is kept covered from camera.

357 INT. CRYPT - MED.

on Yvonne as she recognizes Talbot. Her face lights up and she springs to her feet calling his name. She runs from the scene to climb up to him.

358 INT. CRYPT - MED.

at cave-in. Anatole is looking off in the direction of the stairs. He sees Yvonne run toward them and yells after her.

                    ANATOLE
          Yvonne! Keep away from him.

359 INT. STAIR TOWER - MED. FULL

at foot of stairs. Yvonne runs in from the crypt. She pauses long enough to look back at her father, then ignoring the warning, she turns again and dashes up the steps to the landing where the fight is going on.

360 INT. STAIR TOWER - MED.

on the stair landing. Talbot, back to camera, pushes the two gendarmes back into passage, then drags them both back out with him.

361 INT. STAIR TOWER - MED. PAN

on Yvonne hurrying up the stairs. As Camera brings her up to the landing. Talbot (his identity still hidden from her) knocks the gendarme back into the passageway where he falls unconscious. In almost the same movement, he hurls the other off the landing. The man falls with a wild scream to the stone floor below. The movement swings Talbot around where for the first time the girl can really see him and she stops short a couple of feet from him petrified with horror. For a split second she stands there, then turns to flee back down the stairs. He reaches her in a bound and grabs her.

F:

362 INT. STAIR TOWER - CLOSE

on the werewolf as he swings the girl around and bends to sink his teeth in her throat. He straightens at a shout from o.s.

> ANATOLE'S VOICE (O.S.)
> Stop, Talbot! Remember the silver bullet!

Talbot stares down at the lower floor.

363 INT CRYPT - FULL FROM TALBOT'S ANGLE

Anatole is running toward foot of stairs with the gun held for a quick shot.

364 INT. STAIR TOWER - MED.

at tope of stairs. Talbot has the half-conscious Yvonne held in his arms and is staring down at Anatole with the rile o.s. Now, of course, he doesn't want to be killed. He snatches up the girl, and swinging her between himself and the man below, he starts back toward the passage.

365 INT. STAIR TOWER - FULL

shooting down on Anatole as he raises the rifle, takes deliberate aim and fires.

366 INT. STAIR TOWER - MED.

at entrance to landing. Talbot is moving into the passage-way when the shot gets him. She stops short, stiffening with the shock. Gradually his grip on the girl relaxes and she slowly slides through his arms to the ground. He twists and tries to hang onto the wall for support, while she half rises behind him staring at him frozen with horror. Now his knees fail. He takes a staggering step forward, stops, sways, then pitches forward off the landing.

367 INT. STAIR TOWER - FULL

Anatole in f.g., as Talbot makes the final plunge from the landing above to the stone floor below. Yvonne is seen to get to her full height and start down the stairs leaning weakly against the wall for support

F:

368   INT. STAIR TOWER - CLOSE (TRICK SHOT)

on Talbot lying on the floor. His face is contorting with pain and rage. The wolflike appearance starts to disappear and in the end he becomes Larry Talbot once more, all appearance of viciousness gone from his face. He looks up past camera with a faint smile.

369   INT. STAIR TOWER - MED. CLOSE

on Anatole staring down at Talbot. Yvonne enters to him staring down at Talbot o.s. She speaks his name in a stifled way and drops sobbing beside him, CAMERA TILTING DOWN to a CLOSE SHOT on the two as she buries her face against his breast.

> TALBOT
> (smiling weakly)
> You mustn't Yvonne. Your father only did what I asked him to do.

One arm moves weakly up to her shoulder in a caress as he continues:

> TALBOT
>
> And you brought the only beauty in my life I have ever known - even if it was for so short a time.

His eyes turn up to Anatole o.s. and he adds:

> TALBOT
> (continuing)
> Thanks - friend. Now I can rest in - -

His eyes close and his voice fades away leaving the sentence unfinished. Only the quiet sobbing of the girl can be heard as we

FADE OUT

THE END

www.ingramcontent.com/pod-product-compliance
Lightning Source LLC
Chambersburg PA
CBHW080250170426
43192CB00014BA/2627